THE SCHOOL FOR WIVES
AND
THE LEARNED LADIES

OTHER BOOKS BY RICHARD WILBUR

The Beautiful Changes and Other Poems

Ceremony and Other Poems

A Bestiary (editor, with Alexander Calder)

Molière's *The Misanthrope* (translator)

Things of This World

Poems 1943–1956

Candide (with Lillian Hellman)

Poe: Complete Poems (editor)

Advice to a Prophet and Other Poems

Molière's *Tartuffe* (translator)

The Poems of Richard Wilbur

Loudmouse (for children)

Shakespeare: Poems (co-editor, with Alfred Harbage)

Walking to Sleep: New Poems and Translations

Molière's *The School for Wives* (translator)

Opposites

The Mind-Reader: New Poems

Responses: Prose Pieces, 1953–1976

Molière's *The Learned Ladies* (translator)

Racine's *Andromache* (translator)

Racine's *Phaedra* (translator)

New and Collected Poems

More Opposites

Molière's *The School for Husbands and Sganarelle, or The Imaginary Cuckold* (translator)

Molière's *Amphitryon*

The Catbird's Song: Prose Pieces 1963–1995

Molière's *Tartuffe* (bilingual edition)

JEAN BAPTISTE POQUELIN DE

THE SCHOOL FOR WIVES

AND

THE LEARNED LADIES

TRANSLATED INTO ENGLISH VERSE BY
RICHARD WILBUR

A HARVEST BOOK
HARCOURT, INC.
ORLANDO   AUSTIN   NEW YORK
SAN DIEGO   LONDON

CONTENTS

The School for Wives

I

The Learned Ladies

153

THE SCHOOL FOR WIVES

COMEDY IN FIVE ACTS, 1662

To the memory of
Louis Jouvet
1887–1951

INTRODUCTION

As Dorante says in the *Critique de l'École des femmes*, a comic monster need not lack all attractive qualities. Arnolphe, the hero of Molière's first great verse comedy, is a forty-two-year-old provincial bourgeois whom it is possible to like, up to a point, for his coarse heartiness and his generosity with money. He is, however, a madman, and his alienation is of a harmful and unlovable kind. What ails him is a deep general insecurity, which has somehow been focused into a specific terror of being cuckolded. In fear of that humiliation, he has put off marriage until what, for the seventeenth century, was a very ripe age; meanwhile, he has buttressed his frail vanity by gloating over such of his neighbors as have been deceived by their wives. He has, furthermore, become the guardian of a four-year-old child, Agnès, with a view to shaping her into his idea of a perfect bride, and for thirteen years has had her trained to be docile and ignorant. It is his theory, based upon much anxious observation, that a stupid wife will not shame her husband by infidelity. As the play begins, Arnolphe is about to marry Agnès and achieve a double satisfaction: he will quiet his long trepidation by marrying safely, and he will have the prideful pleasure of showing the world how to rig an infallible alliance. It goes without saying that poor, stultified Agnès is not his object but his victim.

Arnolphe, then, is one of Molière's coercers of life. Like Tartuffe, he proposes to manipulate the world for his own ends, and the play is one long joke about the futility of selfish calculation. Agnès is guileless; her young man, Horace, is a rash bumbler who informs his rival of all that he does and means to do; yet despite Arnolphe's mature canniness, and his twenty years' pondering and plotting, he loses out to a *jeune innocente* and a *jeune écervelé*. Why? There is much high talk in the play, especially from Arnolphe, of cruel

3

destiny, fate, and the stars, and this contributes, as J. D. Hubert has noted, to an effect of "burlesque tragedy"; it is not implacable fate, however, but ridiculous chance which repeatedly spoils Arnolphe's designs. And indeed, the plans of other characters, even when benign, meet constantly with the fortuitous: if Horace achieves his goal, it is certainly not because his blundering intrigues have mastered circumstance; and though Oronte and Enrique accomplish the premeditated union of their children, *le hasard* has already brought the pair together. The play seems to assert that any effort to impose expectations on life will meet with surprises, and that a narrow, rigid, and inhumane demand will not be honored by Nature.

The plot of *L'École des femmes* has often been criticized for its unlikelihood. Doubtless Molière was careless of the fact, since, as W. G. Moore has written, "The plot is not the main thing at all. . . . The high points of the play are not the turning points of the action; they are moments when the clash of youth and age, of spontaneity and automatism, takes shape in speech and scene." And yet it may not be too much to say that the absurdity of the plot is expressive, that it presents us with the world as Arnolphe is bound to experience it. To an obsessed man, the world will be full of exasperating irrelevancies: in this case, a dead kitten, a ribbon, the inopportune chatter of a notary. Similarly, a man who has for years left nothing to chance in the prosecution of a maniacal plan, and who encounters difficulties on the very eve of success, will experience the world as a chaos of disruptive accidents, a storm of casualty: in this case, an old friend's son will by chance gain the affections of Arnolphe's intended; in repeated chance meetings he will subject Arnolphe, whose new title he chances not to know, to tormenting confidences; Oronte and Enrique will chance to arrive in town on what was to have been Arnolphe's wedding day, and will reveal the true identity of the young woman whom Arnolphe once chanced to adopt. It is all too much, for Arnolphe and for us, and in the last-minute breathless summary of Enrique's story, delivered by Chrysalde and Oronte in alternating couplets, Molière both burlesques a species of comic dénouement and acknowledges the outrageousness of his own. At the same time, for this reader, the gay arbitrariness of the close celebrates a truth which is central to the comic vision—that life will not be controlled, but makes a fluent resistance to all crabbèd constraint. The most triumphant demonstration of life's (or Nature's) irrepressibility occurs within Arnolphe himself, when, after so many years of coldly exploiting Agnès for his pride's sake, he becomes vulnerably human by falling in love with her.

Spontaneity versus automatism, life's happy refusal to conform to cranky plans and theories: such terms describe the play for me. Some, however, may wish to be less general, and to discern here a thesis play about, say, education. This comedy is, indeed, permeated with the themes of instruction and learning. Arnolphe has Agnès minimally educated, so that she will have no attractive accomplishments; the nuns teach her to pray, spin, and sew (and somehow, though it is against her guardian's orders, she also learns to read). In Act III, Arnolphe himself becomes her teacher, or, rather, her priest, and with repeated threats of hell-fire informs her that the function of a wife is to live wholly for her husband, in absolute subjection. *The Maxims of Marriage*, which Agnès is then given to study, are likened by Arnolphe to the rules which a novice must learn on entering a convent; and very like they are, counseling as they do a cloistered and sacrificial life devoted to the worship of one's husband. Arnolphe's whole teaching is that the purpose of marriage is to preserve the husband's honor, which is like saying that the purpose of dancing is not to break a leg; and his whole education of Agnès is intended to incapacitate her for adultery by rendering her spiritless and uninteresting. There are moments, I think, when other characters burlesque Arnolphe as educator: the manservant Alain, informing Georgette in Act II, Scene 2 that "womankind is . . . the soup of man," caricatures his master's attitude toward women, as well as his patronizing pedagogical style; and the notary, torrentially instructing Arnolphe in contract law, resembles in his pedantic formulae the Arnolphe of the smug thesis, the airtight plan, and the *Maxims*. Much else in the play might be seen as extending the motif of instruction: Arnolphe rehearsing or drilling his servants; Chrysalde lecturing Arnolphe on the temperate view of cuckoldry; Arnolphe schooling himself in the causes of marital disaster, being guided by a Greek who counseled Augustus, or advising Oronte on the use of paternal power. But what is more surely pertinent, and stands in opposition to Arnolphe's kind of schooling, is the transformation of Horace and Agnès by that *grand maître*, Love. When we first meet him, Horace is a pretty-boy very full of himself and quite capable of seducing Agnès, but by the fifth act he has come to esteem and cherish her, and had "rather die than do her any wrong." Agnès, awakened by love to her own childish ignorance and dependence, proceeds like Juliet to develop gumption and resourcefulness, and discovers a wit which is the more devastating because of her continuing simplicity.

The play is full of "education"; granted. But it cannot convincingly be interpreted as a thesis play *about* education. What can Molière be said to advocate? Latin for women? The inclusion of love in the curriculum? Clearly Molière had a low opinion of Agnès' convent schooling, which was rather standard for the age; what really interests him, however, is not the deficiencies of such schooling but Arnolphe's ill-intended use of them. Similarly, Molière is concerned not with religion but with Arnolphe's selfish and Orgon-like abuse of it, his turning it into a bludgeon. Nor does he comment on parental authority in itself, but, rather, on Arnolphe's attempt to exploit it for his own ends. It will not do, in short, for the contemporary reader or director to inject this play with Student Unrest or Women's Liberation, or to descry in it a Generation Gap. That way lies melo-drama.

Any director of this English version will have to solve for himself certain problems of interpretation and staging, but I shall say what I think. It is my own decided opinion that Chrysalde is *not* a cuckold, and that Arnolphe's second speech in Act I, Scene 1 is a bit of crude and objectionable ribbing. Chrysalde's discourses about cuckoldry should be regarded, I think, both as frequently dubious "reasoning" and as bear-baiting; a good actor would know where to modulate between them. Arnolphe's distaste for fuss and sophistication is likely to impress some as an endearing quality, but I do not see it so; rather, it is of a piece with the man's anxiety to prove himself superior to a society whose ridicule he fears, and like the "honesty" of the *Misanthrope*'s Alceste, it entails posturing and bad faith. Finally, there is the fact that much of the slapstick in the plot—the throwing of the brick, Horace's tumble from the ladder—occurs off stage, and that the on-stage proceedings consist in fair part of long speeches. I should be sorry to see any director right this apparent im-balance by introducing too much pie-throwing and bottom-pinching of his own invention. Once again, Dorante gives Molière's point of view: the long speeches, he says, "are them-selves actions," involving incessant ironic *interplay* between speakers and hearers. To take the most obvious example, Horace's addresses to Arnolphe are rendered wonderfully "busy" by the fact that he does not know he is addressing M. de la Souche, that Arnolphe cannot enlighten him, and that Arnolphe must continually struggle to conceal his glee or anguish. To add any great amount of farcical "business" to such complex comedy would be to divert in an unfortunate sense.

This translation has aimed at a thought-for-thought fidelity, and has sought in its verse to avoid the metronomic, which is particularly fatal on the stage: I have sometimes been very limber indeed, as in the line "He's the most hideous Christian I ever did see." For a few words or phrases I am indebted to earlier English versions in blank verse or prose. I must also thank Jan Miel for helping me to improve these remarks; Robert Hollander, Stephen Porter, and William Jay Smith for reading and criticizing the translation; and John Berryman for encouraging me to undertake it.

CHARACTERS

ARNOLPHE, also known as MONSIEUR DE LA SOUCHE

AGNÈS, an innocent young girl, Arnolphe's ward

HORACE, Agnès' lover, Oronte's son

ALAIN, a peasant, Arnolphe's manservant

GEORGETTE, a peasant woman, servant to Arnolphe

CHRYSALDE, a friend of Arnolphe's

ENRIQUE, Chrysalde's brother-in-law, Agnès' father

ORONTE, Horace's father and Arnolphe's old friend

A NOTARY

The scene is a square in a provincial city.

First produced by the Phoenix Theatre, *New York, on February 16, 1971*

ACT 1

SCENE ONE

CHRYSALDE, ARNOLPHE

CHRYSALDE

So, you're resolved to give this girl your hand?

ARNOLPHE

Tomorrow I shall marry her, as planned.

CHRYSALDE

We're quite alone here, and we can discuss
Your case with no one overhearing us:
Shall I speak openly, and as your friend?
This plan—for your sake—troubles me no end.
I must say that, from every point of view,
Taking a wife is a rash step for you.

ARNOLPHE

You think so? Might it be, friend, that you base
Your fears for me upon your own sad case?
Cuckolds would have us think that all who marry
Acquire a set of horns as corollary.

CHRYSALDE

Fate gives men horns, and fate can't be withstood;
To fret about such matters does no good.
What makes me fear for you is the way you sneer
At every luckless husband of whom you hear.
You know that no poor cuckold, great or small,
Escapes your wit; you mock them one and all,
And take delight in making boisterous mention
Of all intrigues which come to your attention.

ARNOLPHE

Why not? What other town on earth is known
For husbands so long-suffering as our own?
Can we not all too readily bring to mind
Ill-treated dupes of every shape and kind?
One husband's rich; his helpmeet shares the wealth
With paramours who cuckold him by stealth;
Another, with a scarcely kinder fate,
Sees other men heap gifts upon his mate—
Who frees his mind of jealous insecurity
By saying that they're tributes to her purity.
One cuckold impotently storms and rants;
Another mildly bows to circumstance,
And when some gallant calls to see his spouse,
Discreetly takes his hat and leaves the house.
One wife, confiding in her husband, mentions
A swain who bores her with his warm attentions;
The husband smugly pities the poor swain
For all his efforts—which are *not* in vain.
Another wife explains her wealthy state
By saying that she's held good cards of late;
Her husband thanks the Lord and gives Him praise,

Not guessing what bad game she truly plays.
Thus, all about us, there are themes for wit;
May I not, as an observer, jest a bit?
May I not laugh at—

CHRYSALDE

Yes; but remember, do,
That those you mock may someday mock at you.
Now, I hear gossip, I hear what people say
About the latest scandals of the day,
But whatsoever I'm told, I never hear it
With wicked glee and in a gloating spirit.
I keep my counsel; and though I may condemn
Loose wives, and husbands who put up with them,
And though I don't propose, you may be sure,
To endure the wrongs which some weak men endure,
Still, I am never heard to carp and crow,
For tables have been known to turn, you know,
And there's no man who can predict, in fact,
How in such circumstances he would act.
In consequence, should fate bestow on me
What all must fear, the horns of cuckoldry,
The world would treat me gently, I believe,
And be content with laughing up its sleeve.
There are, in fact, some kindly souls who might
Commiserate me in my sorry plight.
But you, dear fellow, with you it's not the same.
I say once more, you play a dangerous game.
Since with your jeering tongue you plague the lives
Of men who are unlucky in their wives,
And persecute them like a fiend from Hell,
Take care lest someday you be jeered as well.
If the least whisper about your wife were heard,

They'd mock you from the housetops, mark my word.
What's more—

ARNOLPHE

Don't worry, friend; I'm not a fool.
I shan't expose myself to ridicule.
I know the tricks and ruses, shrewd and sly,
Which wives employ, and cheat their husbands by;
I know that women can be deep and clever;
But I've arranged to be secure forever:
So simple is the girl I'm going to wed
That I've no fear of horns upon my head.

CHRYSALDE

Simple! You mean to bind yourself for life—

ARNOLPHE

A man's not simple to take a simple wife.
Your wife, no doubt, is a wise, virtuous woman,
But brightness, as a rule, is a bad omen,
And I know men who've undergone much pain
Because they married girls with too much brain.
I want no intellectual, if you please,
Who'll talk of nothing but her Tuesday teas,
Who'll frame lush sentiments in prose and verse
And fill the house with wits, and fops, and worse,
While I, as her dull husband, stand about
Like a poor saint whose candles have gone out.
No, keep your smart ones; I've no taste for such.
Women who versify know far too much.
I want a wife whose thought is not sublime,

Who has no notion what it is to rhyme,
And who, indeed, if she were asked in some
Insipid parlor game, "What rhymes with drum?"
Would answer in all innocence, "A fife."
In short, I want an unaccomplished wife,
And there are four things only she must know:
To say her prayers, love me, spin, and sew.

CHRYSALDE

Stupidity's your cup of tea, I gather.

ARNOLPHE

I'd choose an ugly, stupid woman rather
Than a great beauty who was over-wise.

CHRYSALDE

But wit and beauty—

ARNOLPHE

Virtue is what I prize.

CHRYSALDE

But how can you expect an idiot
To know what's virtuous and what is not?
Not only would it be a lifelong bore
To have a senseless wife, but what is more,
I hardly think you could depend upon her
To guard her husband's forehead from dishonor.
If a bright woman breaks her wedding vow,

She knows what she is doing, anyhow;
A simpleton, however, can commit
Adultery without suspecting it.

ARNOLPHE

To that fine argument I can but say
What Pantagruel says in Rabelais:
Preach and harangue from now till Whitsuntide
Against my preference for a stupid bride;
You'll be amazed to find, when you have ceased,
That I've not been persuaded in the least.

CHRYSALDE

So be it.

ARNOLPHE

Each man has his own design
For wedded bliss, and I shall follow mine.
I'm rich, and so can take a wife who'll be
Dependent, in the least respect, on me—
A sweet, submissive girl who cannot claim
To have brought me riches or an ancient name.
The gentle, meek expression which she wore
Endeared Agnès to me when she was four;
Her mother being poor, I felt an urge
To make the little thing my ward and charge,
And the good peasant woman was most pleased
To grant my wish, and have her burden eased.
In a small convent, far from the haunts of man,
The girl was reared according to my plan:
I told the nuns what means must be employed
To keep her growing mind a perfect void,

18

[Act One · Scene One]

And, God be praised, they had entire success.
As a grown girl, her simple-mindedness
Is such that I thank Heaven for granting me
A bride who suits my wishes to a T.
She's out of the convent now, and since my gate
Stands open to society, early and late,
I keep her here, in another house I own,
Where no one calls, and she can be alone:
And, to protect her artless purity,
I've hired two servants as naïve as she.
I've told you all this so that you'll understand
With what great care my marriage has been planned;
And now, to clinch my story, I invite
You, my dear friend, to dine with her tonight;
I want you to examine her, and decide
Whether or not my choice is justified.

CHRYSALDE

Delighted.

ARNOLPHE

You'll gain, I think, a lively sense
Of her sweet person and her innocence.

CHRYSALDE

As to her innocence, what you've related
Leaves little doubt—

ARNOLPHE

My friend, 't was understated.
Her utter naïveté keeps me in stitches.

19

I laugh so that I almost burst my breeches.
You won't believe this, but the other day
She came and asked me in a puzzled way,
And with a manner touchingly sincere,
If children are begotten through the ear.

CHRYSALDE

I'm happy indeed, Monsieur Arnolphe—

ARNOLPHE

For shame!
Why must you always use my former name?

CHRYSALDE

I'm used to it, I suppose. What's more, I find
That *de la Souche* forever slips my mind.
What in the devil has persuaded you
To debaptize yourself at forty-two
And take a lordly title which you base
On an old tree stump at your country place?

ARNOLPHE

The name La Souche goes with the property
And sounds much better than Arnolphe to me.

CHRYSALDE

But why forsake the name your fathers bore
For one that's fantasy and nothing more?
Yet lately that's become the thing to do.

I am reminded—no offense to you—
Of a peasant named Gros-Pierre, who owned a small
Parcel of land, an acre or so in all;
He dug a muddy ditch around the same
And took Monsieur de l'Isle for his new name.

ARNOLPHE

I can dispense with stories of that kind.
My name is de la Souche, if you don't mind.
I like that title, and it's mine by right;
To address me otherwise is impolite.

CHRYSALDE

Your new name is employed by few, at best;
Much of your mail, I've noticed, comes addressed—

ARNOLPHE

I don't mind that, from such as haven't been told;
But you—

CHRYSALDE

Enough. Enough. No need to scold.
I hereby promise that, at our next meeting,
"Good day, Monsieur de la Souche" shall be my greeting.

ARNOLPHE

Farewell. I'm going to knock now on my door
And let them know that I'm in town once more.

[*Act One · Scene One*]

CHRYSALDE, *aside, as he moves off*

The man's quite mad. A lunatic, in fact.

ARNOLPHE, *alone*

On certain subjects he's a trifle cracked.
It's curious to see with what devotion
A man will cling to some quite pointless notion.
Ho, there!

SCENE TWO

ALAIN, GEORGETTE, ARNOLPHE

ALAIN, *within*

Who's knocking?

ARNOLPHE

Ho! (*Aside:*) They'll greet me, after
My ten days' trip, with smiles and happy laughter.

ALAIN

Who's there?

ARNOLPHE

It's I.

ALAIN

Georgette!

GEORGETTE

What?

[*Act One · Scene Two*]

ALAIN

Open below!

GEORGETTE

Do it yourself!

ALAIN

You do it!

GEORGETTE

I won't go!

ALAIN

I won't go either!

ARNOLPHE

Gracious servants, these,
To leave me standing here. Ho! If you please!

GEORGETTE

Who's there?

ARNOLPHE

Your master.

[*Act One · Scene Two*]

GEORGETTE

Alain!

ALAIN

What?

GEORGETTE

Go lift the latch!

It's him.

ALAIN

You do it.

GEORGETTE

I'm getting the fire to catch.

ALAIN

I'm keeping the cat from eating the canary.

ARNOLPHE

Whoever doesn't admit me, and in a hurry,
Will get no food for four long days, and more.
Aha!

GEORGETTE

I'll get it; what are you coming for?

[*Act One · Scene Two*]

ALAIN

Why you, not me? That's a sneaky trick to play!

GEORGETTE

Get out of the way.

ALAIN

No, *you* get out of the way.

GEORGETTE

I want to open that door.

ALAIN

I want to, too.

GEORGETTE

You won't.

ALAIN

And you won't either.

GEORGETTE

Neither will you.

ARNOLPHE, *to himself*

My patience with these two amazes me.

[*Act One · Scene Two*]

ALAIN

I've opened the door, Sir.

GEORGETTE

No, I did it! See?
'T was I.

ALAIN

If only the master, here, weren't present,
I'd—

ARNOLPHE, *receiving a blow from Alain, meant for Georgette*

Blast you!

ALAIN

Sorry, Sir.

ARNOLPHE

You clumsy peasant!

ALAIN

It's her fault too, Sir.

ARNOLPHE

Both of you, stop this row.
I want to question you; no nonsense, now.
Alain, is everything going smoothly here?

[*Act One · Scene Two*]

ALAIN

Well, Sir, we're—
    (*Arnolphe removes Alain's hat; Alain
    obliviously puts it back on.*)
        Well, Sir—
        (*Hat business again.*)
           Well, thank God, Sir, we're—
    (*Arnolphe removes Alain's hat a third time,
    and throws it to the ground.*)

ARNOLPHE

Where did you learn, you lout, to wear a hat
While talking to your master? Answer me that.

ALAIN

You're right, I'm wrong.

ARNOLPHE

           Now, have Agnès come down.
  (*To Georgette:*)
Was she unhappy while I was out of town?

GEORGETTE

Unhappy? No.

ARNOLPHE

    No?

28

[*Act One · Scene Two*]

Yes.

ARNOLPHE

For what reason, then?

GEORGETTE

Well, she kept thinking you'd be back again,
So that whatever passed on the avenue—
Horse, mule, or ass—she thought it must be you.

SCENE THREE

ARNOLPHE

Her needlework in hand! That's a good sign.
Well, well, Agnès, I'm back and feeling fine.
Are you glad to see me?

AGNÈS

Oh, yes, Sir; thank the Lord.

ARNOLPHE

I'm glad to see you too, my little ward.
I take it everything has been all right?

AGNÈS

Except for the fleas, which bothered me last night.

ARNOLPHE

Well, there'll be someone soon to drive them away.

AGNÈS

I shall be glad of that.

[*Act One · Scene Three*]

ARNOLPHE

Yes, I dare say.
What are you making?

AGNÈS

A headpiece, Sir, for me;
Your nightshirts are all finished, as you'll see.

ARNOLPHE

Excellent. Well, upstairs with you, my dear:
I'll soon come back and see you, never fear;
There's serious talk in which we must engage.
        (*Exeunt all but Arnolphe.*)
O learned ladies, heroines of the age,
Gushers of sentiment, I say that you,
For all your verse, and prose, and billets-doux,
Your novels, and your bright accomplishments,
Can't match this good and modest ignorance.

SCENE FOUR

HORACE, ARNOLPHE

ARNOLPHE

What does her lack of money matter to me?
What matters— Oh! What's this? No! Can it be?
I'm dreaming. Yes, it's he, my dear friend's boy.
Well!

HORACE

Sir!

ARNOLPHE

Horace!

HORACE

Arnolphe!

ARNOLPHE

Ah, what a joy!
How long have you been in town?

32

HORACE

Nine days.

ARNOLPHE

Ah, so.

HORACE

I called at your house, in vain, a week ago.

ARNOLPHE

I'd left for the country.

HORACE

Yes, you were three days gone.

ARNOLPHE

How quickly children grow! How time rolls on!
I am amazed that you're so big and tall.
I can remember when you were—
    (*He makes a gesture of measuring from the floor.*)
                that small.

HORACE

Yes, time goes by.

ARNOLPHE

But come now, tell me of
Oronte, your father, whom I esteem and love:

33

How's my old friend? Still spry and full of zest?
In all that's his, I take an interest.
Alas, it's four years since I talked with him,
And we've not written in the interim.

HORACE

Seigneur Arnolphe, he's spry enough for two;
He gave me this little note to give to you,
But now he writes me that he's coming here
Himself, for reasons not entirely clear.
Some fellow-townsman of yours, whom you may know,
Went to America fourteen years ago;
He's come back rich. Do you know of whom I speak?

ARNOLPHE

No. Did the letter give his name?

HORACE

                    Enrique.

ARNOLPHE

No . . . no . . .

HORACE

                    My father writes as if I ought
To recognize that name, but I do not.
He adds that he and Enrique will soon set out
On some great errand that he's vague about.

ARNOLPHE

I long to see your father, that sterling man.
I'll welcome him as royally as I can.
    (*He reads the note from Oronte.*)
A friendly letter needn't flatter and fuss.
All this politeness is superfluous,
And even without his asking, I'd have desired
To lend you any money you required.

HORACE

I'll take you at your word, Sir. Can you advance
Fifty *pistoles* or so, by any chance?

ARNOLPHE

I'm grateful that you let me be of use,
And what you ask, I happily can produce.
Just keep the purse.

HORACE

Here—

ARNOLPHE

                Forget the I.O.U.
Now, how does our town impress you? Tell me, do.

HORACE

It's rich in people, sublime in architecture,
And full of fine amusements, I conjecture.

35

ARNOLPHE

There's pleasure here for every taste; and those
The world calls gallants, ladies' men, or beaux
Find here the sport on which their hearts are set,
Since every woman in town's a born coquette.
Our ladies, dark or fair, are pliant creatures;
Their husbands, likewise, have permissive natures;
Oh, it's a capital game; it's often made
Me double up with mirth to see it played.
But you've already broken some hearts, I'd guess;
Have you no gallant conquest to confess?
Cuckolds are made by such as you, young man,
And looks like yours buy more than money can.

HORACE

Well, since you ask, I'll lay my secrets bare.
I *have* been having a covert love affair—
Which, out of friendship, I shall now unveil.

ARNOLPHE

Good, good; 't will be another rakish tale
Which I can put into my repertory.

HORACE

Sir, I must beg you: don't divulge my story.

ARNOLPHE

Of course not.

[*Act One · Scene Four*]

HORACE

       As you know, Sir, in these matters,
One word let slip can leave one's hopes in tatters.
To put the business plainly, then, my heart's
Been lost to a lady dwelling in these parts.
My overtures, I'm very pleased to state,
Have found her ready to reciprocate,
And not to boast, or slur her reputation,
I think I'm in a hopeful situation.

ARNOLPHE, *laughing*

Who is she?

HORACE

       A girl whose beauty is past telling,
And yonder red-walled mansion is her dwelling.
She's utterly naïve, because a blind
Fool has sequestered her from humankind,
And yet, despite the ignorance in which
He keeps her, she has charms that can bewitch;
She's most engaging, and conveys a sense
Of sweetness against which there's no defense.
But you, perhaps, have seen this star of love
Whose many graces I'm enamoured of.
Her name's Agnès.

ARNOLPHE, *aside*

Oh, death!

37

[*Act One · Scene Four*]

HORACE

> The man, I hear,
> Is called La Zousse, La Source, or something queer;
> I didn't pay much attention to the name.
> He's rich, I gather, but his wits are lame,
> And he's accounted a ridiculous fellow.
> D'you know him?

ARNOLPHE, *aside*

> Ugh, what a bitter pill to swallow!

HORACE

> I said, do you know him?

ARNOLPHE

> Yes, I do, in a way.

HORACE

> He's a dolt, isn't he?

ARNOLPHE

> Oh!

HORACE

> What? What did you say?
> He is, I take it. And a jealous idiot, too?
> An ass? I see that all they said was true.

Well, to repeat, I love Agnès, a girl
Who is, to say the least, an orient pearl,
And it would be a sin for such a treasure
To be subjected to that old fool's pleasure.
Henceforth, my thoughts and efforts shall combine
To break his jealous hold and make her mine;
This purse, which I made bold to borrow, will lend
Me great assistance toward that worthy end.
As you well know, whatever means one tries,
Money's the key to every enterprise,
And this sweet metal, which all men hanker for,
Promotes our conquests, whether in love or war.
You look disturbed, Sir; can it be that you
Do not approve of what I mean to do?

ARNOLPHE

No; I was thinking—

HORACE

       I'm boring you. Farewell, then.
I'll soon drop by, to express my thanks again.

ARNOLPHE, *to himself*

How could this happen—

HORACE, *returning*

       Again, Sir, I entreat
You not to tell my secret; be discreet.
    (*He leaves.*)

[*Act One* · *Scene Four*]

ARNOLPHE, *to himself*

I'm thunderstruck.

HORACE, *returning*

          Above all, don't inform
My father; he might raise a dreadful storm.
      (*He leaves.*)

ARNOLPHE (*He expects Horace to return again;
that not occurring, he talks to himself.*)

Oh! . . . What I've suffered during this conversation!
No soul has ever endured such agitation.
With what imprudence, and how hastily
He came and told the whole affair . . . to me!
He didn't know I'd taken a new title;
Still, what a rash and blundering recital!
I should, however, have kept myself in hand,
So as to learn what strategy he's planned,
And prompt his indiscretion, and discover
To what extent he has become her lover.
Come, I'll catch up with him; he can't be far;
I'll learn from him precisely how things are.
Alas, I'm trembling; I fear some further blow;
One can discover more than one wants to know.

ACT 2

SCENE ONE

ARNOLPHE

It's just as well, no doubt, that I should fail
To catch him—that I somehow lost his trail:
For I could not have managed to dissemble
The turbulence of soul which makes me tremble;
He'd have perceived my present near-despair,
Of which it's best that he be unaware.
But I'm not one to be resigned and meek
And turn this little fop the other cheek.
I'll stop him; and the first thing I must do
Is find out just how far they've gone, those two.
This matter involves my honor, which I prize;
The girl's my wife already, in my eyes;
If she's been tarnished, I am covered with shame,
And all she's done reflects on my good name.
Oh, why did I take that trip? Oh, dear, oh, dear.
                    (*He knocks at his door.*)

SCENE TWO

ALAIN, GEORGETTE, ARNOLPHE

ALAIN

Ah! *This* time, Sir—

ARNOLPHE

Hush! Both of you come here:
This way, this way. Come, hurry! Do as you're told!

GEORGETTE

You frighten me; you make my blood run cold.

ARNOLPHE

So! In my absence, you have disobeyed me!
The two of you, in concert, have betrayed me!

GEORGETTE, *falling on her knees*

Don't eat me, Sir; don't eat me alive, I beg.

ALAIN, *aside*

I'd swear some mad dog's nipped him in the leg.

44

[*Act Two · Scene Two*]

ARNOLPHE, *aside*

Oof! I'm too tense to speak. I'd like to shed
These blasted clothes. I'm burning up with dread.
       (*To Alain and Georgette:*)
You cursèd scoundrels, while I was gone you let
A man into this house—
       (*To Alain, who has made a move to flee:*)
                  No, not just yet!
Tell me at once— (*To Georgette:*) Don't move! I want
 you two
To tell me— Whff! I mean to learn from you—
       (*Alain and Georgette rise and try to escape.*)
If anyone moves, I'll squash him like a louse.
Now tell me, how did that man get into my house?
Well, speak! Come, hurry. Quickly! Time is fleeting!
Let's hear it! Speak!

ALAIN *and* GEORGETTE, *falling on their knees*

Oh! Oh!

GEORGETTE

My heart's stopped beating.

ALAIN

I'm dying.

ARNOLPHE, *aside*

I'm sweating, and I need some air.
I must calm down: I'll walk around the square.

45

When I saw him in his cradle, I didn't know
What he'd grow up and do to me. O woe!
Perhaps—yes, I'd do better to receive
The truth from her own lips, I now believe.
I'll mute my rage as well I know how;
Patience, my wounded heart! Beat softly, now!
    (*To Alain and Georgette:*)
Get up, and go inside, and call Agnès.
Wait. (*Aside:*) That way her surprise would be the less.
They'd warn her of my anger, I don't doubt.
I'd best go in myself and bring her out.
    (*To Alain and Georgette:*)
Wait here.

SCENE THREE

ALAIN, GEORGETTE

GEORGETTE

God help us, but his rage is terrible!
The way he glared at me—it was unbearable.
He's the most hideous Christian I ever did see.

ALAIN

He's vexed about that man, as I said he'd be.

GEORGETTE

But why does he order us, with barks and roars,
Never to let the mistress go outdoors?
Why does he want us to conceal her here
From all the world, and let no man come near?

ALAIN

It's jealousy that makes him treat her so.

GEORGETTE

But how did he get like that, I'd like to know?

[*Act Two · Scene Three*]

ALAIN

It comes of being jealous, I assume.

GEORGETTE

But why is he jealous? Why must he rage and fume?

ALAIN

Well, jealousy—listen carefully, Georgette—
Is a thing—a thing—which makes a man upset,
And makes him close his doors to everyone.
I'm going to give you a comparison,
So that you'll clearly understand the word.
Suppose you were eating soup, and it occurred
That someone tried to take what you were eating:
Wouldn't you feel like giving him a beating?

GEORGETTE

Yes, I see that.

ALAIN

        Then grasp this, if you can.
Womankind is, in fact, the soup of man,
And when a man perceives that others wish
To dip their dirty fingers into his dish,
His temper flares, and bursts into a flame.

GEORGETTE

Yes. But not everybody feels the same.
Some husbands seem to be delighted when
Their wives consort with fancy gentlemen.

ALAIN

Not every husband is the greedy kind
That wants to have it all.

GEORGETTE

          If I'm not blind,
He's coming back.

ALAIN

It's he; your eyes are keen.

GEORGETTE

He's scowling.

ALAIN

That's because he's feeling mean.

SCENE FOUR

ARNOLPHE, *aside*

A certain Greek presumed once to advise
The great Augustus, and his words were wise:
When you are vexed, he said, do not forget,
Before you act, to say the alphabet,
So as to cool your temper, and prevent
Rash moves which later on you might repent.
In dealing with Agnès, I have applied
That counsel, and I've bidden her come outside,
Under the pretext of a morning stroll,
So that I can relieve my jangled soul
By seeking dulcetly to draw her out
And learn the truth, and put an end to doubt.
(*Calling:*) Come out, Agnès. (*To Alain and Georgette:*)
    Go in.

SCENE FIVE

ARNOLPHE, AGNÈS

ARNOLPHE

The weather's mild.

AGNÈS

Oh, yes.

ARNOLPHE

Most pleasant.

AGNÈS

Indeed!

ARNOLPHE

What news, my child?

AGNÈS

The kitten died.

[*Act Two · Scene Five*]

ARNOLPHE

Too bad, but what of that?
All men are mortal, my dear, and so's a cat.
While I was gone, no doubt it rained and poured?

AGNÈS

No.

ARNOLPHE

You were bored, perhaps?

AGNÈS

I'm never bored.

ARNOLPHE

During my ten days' absence, what did you do?

AGNÈS

Six nightshirts, I believe; six nightcaps, too.

ARNOLPHE, *after a pause*

My dear Agnès, this world's a curious thing.
What wicked talk one hears, what gossiping!
While I was gone, or so the neighbors claim,
There was a certain strange young man who came
To call upon you here, and was received.
But such a slander's not to be believed,
And I would wager that their so-called news—

AGNÈS

Heavens! Don't wager; you'd be sure to lose.

ARNOLPHE

What! Is it true, then, that a man—

AGNÈS

Oh, yes.
In fact, he all but lived at this address.

ARNOLPHE, *aside*

That frank reply would seem to demonstrate
That she's still free of guile, at any rate.
    (*Aloud:*)
But I gave orders, Agnès, as I recall,
That you were to see no one, no one at all.

AGNÈS

I disobeyed you, but when I tell you why,
You'll say that you'd have done the same as I.

ARNOLPHE

Perhaps; well, tell me how this thing occurred.

AGNÈS

It's the most amazing story you ever heard.
I was sewing, out on the balcony, in the breeze,

When I noticed someone strolling under the trees.
It was a fine young man, who caught my eye
And made me a deep bow as he went by.
I, not to be convicted of a lack
Of manners, very quickly nodded back.
At once, the young man bowed to me again.
I bowed to him a second time, and then
It wasn't very long until he made
A third deep bow, which I of course repaid.
He left, but kept returning, and as he passed,
He'd bow, each time, more gracefully than the last,
While I, observing as he came and went,
Gave each new bow a fresh acknowledgment.
Indeed, had night not fallen, I declare
I think that I might still be sitting there,
And bowing back each time he bowed to me,
For fear he'd think me less polite than he.

ARNOLPHE

Go on.

AGNÈS

Then an old woman came, next day,
And found me standing in the entryway.
She said to me, "May Heaven bless you, dear,
And keep you beautiful for many a year.
God, who bestowed on you such grace and charm,
Did not intend those gifts to do men harm,
And you should know that there's a heart which bears
A wound which you've inflicted unawares."

[*Act Two · Scene Five*]

Old witch! Old tool of Satan! Damn her hide!

AGNÈS

"You say I've wounded somebody?" I cried.
"Indeed you have," she said. "The victim's he
Whom yesterday you saw from the balcony."
"But how could such a thing occur?" I said;
"Can I have dropped some object on his head?"
"No," she replied, "your bright eyes dealt the blow;
Their glances are the cause of all his woe."
"Good heavens, Madam," said I in great surprise,
"Is there some dread contagion in my eyes?"
"Ah, yes, my child," said she. "Your eyes dispense,
Unwittingly, a fatal influence:
The poor young man has dwindled to a shade;
And if you cruelly deny him aid,
I greatly fear," the kind old woman went on,
"That two days more will see him dead and gone."
"Heavens," I answered, "that would be sad indeed.
But what can I do for him? What help does he need?"
"My child," said she, "he only asks of you
The privilege of a little interview;
It is your eyes alone which now can save him,
And cure him of the malady they gave him."
"If that's the case," I said, "I can't refuse;
I'll gladly see him, whenever he may choose."

ARNOLPHE, *aside*

O "kind old woman"! O vicious sorceress!
May Hell reward you for your cleverness!

AGNÈS

And so I saw him, which brought about his cure.
You'll grant I did the proper thing, I'm sure.
How could I have the conscience to deny
The succor he required, and let him die—
I, who so pity anyone in pain,
And cannot bear to see a chicken slain?

ARNOLPHE, *aside*

It's clear that she has meant no wrong, and I
Must blame that foolish trip I took, whereby
I left her unprotected from the lies
That rascally seducers can devise.
Oh, what if that young wretch, with one bold stroke,
Has compromised her? That would be no joke.

AGNÈS

What's wrong? You seem a trifle irritated.
Was there some harm in what I just related?

ARNOLPHE

No, but go on. I want to hear it all.
What happened when the young man came to call?

AGNÈS

Oh, if you'd seen how happy he was, how gay,
And how his sickness vanished right away,
And the jewel-case he gave me—not to forget
The coins he gave to Alain and to Georgette,
You would have loved him also, and you too—

[*Act Two · Scene Five*]

ARNOLPHE

And when you were alone, what did he do?

AGNÈS

He swore he loved me with a matchless passion,
And said to me, in the most charming fashion,
Things which I found incomparably sweet,
And never tire of hearing him repeat,
So much do they delight my ear, and start
I know not what commotion in my heart.

ARNOLPHE, *aside*

O strange interrogation, where each reply
Makes the interrogator wish to die!
    (*To Agnès:*)
Besides these compliments, these sweet addresses,
Were there not also kisses, and caresses?

AGNÈS

Oh, yes! He took my hands, and kissed and kissed
Them both, as if he never would desist.

ARNOLPHE

And did he not take—something else as well?
    (*He notes that she is taken aback.*)
Agh!

AGNÈS

    Well, he—

[*Act Two · Scene Five*]

ARNOLPHE

Yes?

AGNÈS

Took—

ARNOLPHE

What?

AGNÈS

I dare not tell.
I fear that you'll be furious with me.

ARNOLPHE

No.

AGNÈS

Yes.

ARNOLPHE

No, no.

AGNÈS

Then promise not to be.

ARNOLPHE

I promise.

58

AGNÈS

He took my—oh, you'll have a fit.

ARNOLPHE

No.

AGNÈS

Yes.

ARNOLPHE

No, no. The devil! Out with it!
What did he take from you?

AGNÈS

He took—

ARNOLPHE, *aside*

God save me!

AGNÈS

He took the pretty ribbon that you gave me.
Indeed, he begged so that I couldn't resist.

ARNOLPHE, *taking a deep breath*

Forget the ribbon. Tell me: once he'd kissed
Your hands, what else did he do, as you recall?

AGNÈS

Does one do other things?

ARNOLPHE

           No, not at all;
But didn't he ask some further medicine
For the sad state of health that he was in?

AGNÈS

Why, no. But had he asked, you may be sure
I'd have done anything to speed his cure.

ARNOLPHE, *aside*

I've got off cheap this once, thanks be to God;
If I slip again, let all men call me clod.
    (*To Agnès:*)
Agnès, my dear, your innocence is vast;
I shan't reproach you; what is past is past.
But all that trifler wants to do—don't doubt it—
Is to deceive you, and then boast about it.

AGNÈS

Oh, no. He's often assured me otherwise.

ARNOLPHE

Ah, you don't know how that sort cheats and lies.
But do grasp this: to accept a jewel-case,
And let some coxcomb praise your pretty face,

And be complaisant when he takes a notion
To kiss your hands and fill you with "commotion"
Is a great sin, for which your soul could die.

AGNÈS

A sin, you say! But please, Sir, tell me why.

ARNOLPHE

Why? Why? Because, as all authority states,
It's just such deeds that Heaven abominates.

AGNÈS

Abominates! But why should Heaven feel so?
It's all so charming and so sweet, you know!
I never knew about this sort of thing
Till now, or guessed what raptures it could bring.

ARNOLPHE

Yes, all these promises of love undying,
These sighs, these kisses, are most gratifying,
But they must be enjoyed in the proper way;
One must be married first, that is to say.

AGNÈS

And once you're married, there's no evil in it?

ARNOLPHE

That's right.

[*Act Two · Scene Five*]

AGNÈS

Oh, let me marry, then, this minute!

ARNOLPHE

If that's what you desire, I feel the same;
It was to plan your marriage that I came.

AGNÈS

What! Truly?

ARNOLPHE

Yes.

AGNÈS

How happy I shall be!

ARNOLPHE

Yes, wedded life will please you, I foresee.

AGNÈS

You really intend that we two—

ARNOLPHE

Yes, I do.

[*Act Two · Scene Five*]

AGNÈS

Oh, how I'll kiss you if that dream comes true!

ARNOLPHE

And I'll return your kisses, every one.

AGNÈS

I'm never sure when people are making fun.
Are you quite serious?

ARNOLPHE

Yes, I'm serious. Quite.

AGNÈS

We're to be married?

ARNOLPHE

Yes.

AGNÈS

But when?

ARNOLPHE

Tonight.

63

[*Act Two* · *Scene Five*]

AGNÈS, *laughing*

Tonight?

ARNOLPHE

Tonight. It seems you're moved to laughter.

AGNÈS

Yes.

ARNOLPHE

Well, to see you happy is what I'm after.

AGNÈS

Oh, Sir, I owe you more than I can express!
With him, my life will be pure happiness!

ARNOLPHE

With whom?

AGNÈS

With . . . him.

ARNOLPHE

With *him!* Well, think again.
You're rather hasty in your choice of men.
It's quite another husband I have in mind;

And as for "him," as you call him, be so kind,
Regardless of his pitiable disease,
As never again to see him, if you please.
When next he calls, girl, put him in his place
By slamming the door directly in his face;
Then, if he knocks, go up and drop a brick
From the second-floor window. That should do the trick.
Do you understand, Agnès? I shall be hidden
Nearby, to see that you do as you are bidden.

AGNÈS

Oh, dear, he's so good-looking, so—

ARNOLPHE

Be still!

AGNÈS

I just won't have the heart—

ARNOLPHE

Enough; you will.
Now go upstairs.

AGNÈS

How can you—

ARNOLPHE

Do as I say.
I'm master here; I've spoken; go, obey.

ACT 3

SCENE ONE

ARNOLPHE

Yes, I'm most pleased; it couldn't have gone better.
By following my instructions to the letter,
You've put that young philanderer to flight:
See how wise generalship can set things right.
Your innocence had been abused, Agnès;
Unwittingly, you'd got into a mess,
And, lacking my good counsel, you were well
Embarked upon a course which leads to Hell.
Those beaux are all alike, believe you me:
They've ribbons, plumes, and ruffles at the knee,
Fine wigs, and polished talk, and brilliant teeth,
But they're all scales and talons underneath—
Indeed, they're devils of the vilest sort,
Who prey on women's honor for their sport.
However, owing to my watchful care,
You have emerged intact from this affair.
The firm and righteous way in which you threw
That brick at him, and dashed his hopes of you,
Persuades me that there's no cause to delay
The wedding which I promised you today.
But first, it would be well for me to make
A few remarks for your improvement's sake.
    (*To Alain, who brings a chair:*)

I'll sit here, where it's cool.
    (*To Georgette:*) Remember, now—

GEORGETTE

Oh, Sir, we won't forget again, I vow.
That young man won't get round us any more.

ALAIN

I'll give up drink if he gets through that door.
Anyway, he's an idiot; we bit
Two coins he gave us, and they were counterfeit.

ARNOLPHE

Well, go and buy the food for supper, and then
One of you, as you're coming home again,
Can fetch the local notary from the square.
Tell him that there's a contract to prepare.

ARNOLPHE, *seated*

Agnès, stop knitting and hear what I have to say.
Lift up your head a bit, and turn this way.
    (*Putting his finger to his forehead:*)
Look at me *there* while I talk to you, right *there*,
And listen to my every word with care.
My dear, I'm going to wed you, and you should bless
Your vast good fortune and your happiness.
Reflect upon your former low estate,
And judge, then, if my goodness is not great
In raising you, a humble peasant lass,
To be a matron of the middle class,
To share the bed and the connubial bliss
Of one who's shunned the married state till this,
Withholding from a charming score or two
The honor which he now bestows on you.
Be ever mindful, Agnès, that you would be,
Without this union, a nonentity;
And let that thought incline your heart to merit
The name which I shall lend you, and to bear it
With such propriety that I shall never
Regret my choice for any cause whatever.
Marriage, Agnès, is no light matter; the role
Of wife requires austerity of soul,

And I do not exalt you to that station
To lead a life of heedless dissipation.
Yours is the weaker sex, please realize;
It is the beard in which all power lies,
And though there are two portions of mankind,
Those portions are not equal, you will find:
One half commands, the other must obey;
The second serves the first in every way;
And that obedience which the soldier owes
His general, or the loyal servant shows
His master, or the good child pays his sire,
Or the stern abbot looks for in the friar,
Is nothing to the pure docility,
The deep submission and humility
Which a good wife must ever exhibit toward
The man who is her master, chief, and lord.
Should he regard her with a serious air,
She must avert her eyes, and never dare
To lift them to his face again, unless
His look should change to one of tenderness.
Such things aren't understood by women today,
But don't let bad example lead you astray.
Don't emulate those flirts whose indiscretions
Are told all over town at gossip-sessions,
Or yield to Satan's trickery by allowing
Young fops to please you with their smiles and bowing.
Remember that, in marrying, I confide
To you, Agnès, my honor and my pride;
That honor is a tender, fragile thing
With which there can be no light dallying;
And that all misbehaving wives shall dwell
In ever-boiling cauldrons down in Hell.
These are no idle lessons which I impart,
And you'll do well to get them all by heart.

Your soul, if you observe them, and abjure
Flirtation, will be lily-white and pure;
But deviate from honor, and your soul
Will forthwith grow as vile and black as coal;
All will abhor you as a thing of evil,
Till one day you'll be taken by the Devil,
And Hell's eternal fire is where he'll send you—
From which sad fate may Heaven's grace defend you.
Make me a curtsey. Now then, just as a novice,
Entering the convent, learns by heart her office,
So, entering wedlock, you should do the same.
(*He rises.*)
I have, in my pocket, a book of no small fame
From which you'll learn the office of a wife.
'T was written by some man of pious life.
Study his teaching faithfully, and heed it.
Here, take the book; let's hear how well you read it.

AGNÈS, *reading*

The Maxims of Marriage
or
The Duties of a Married Woman,
Together with Her Daily Exercises.

First Maxim:
A woman who in church has said
She'll love and honor and obey
Should get it firmly in her head,
Despite the fashions of the day,
That he who took her for his own
Has taken her for his bed alone.

ARNOLPHE

I shall explain that; doubtless you're perplexed.
But, for the present, let us hear what's next.

AGNÈS, *continuing*

Second Maxim:
She needs no fine attire
More than he may desire
Who is her lord and master.
To dress for any taste but his is vain;
If others find her plain,
'T is no disaster.

Third Maxim:
Let her not daub her face
With paint and patch and powder-base
And creams which promise beauty on the label.
It is not for their husbands' sake
But vanity's, that women undertake
The labors of the dressing table.

Fourth Maxim:
Let her be veiled whenever she leaves the house,
So that her features are obscure and dim.
If she desires to please her spouse,
She must please no one else but him.

Fifth Maxim:
Except for friends who call
To see her husband, let her not admit
Anyone at all.

A visitor whose end
Is to amuse the wife with gallant wit
Is *not* the husband's friend.

Sixth Maxim:

To men who would confer kind gifts upon her,
She must reply with self-respecting nays.
Not to refuse would be to court dishonor.
Nothing is given for nothing nowadays.

Seventh Maxim:

She has no need, whatever she may think,
Of writing table, paper, pen, or ink.
In a proper house, the husband is the one
To do whatever writing's to be done.

Eighth Maxim:

At those licentious things
Called social gatherings,
Wives are corrupted by the worldly crowd.
Since, at such functions, amorous plots are laid
And married men betrayed,
They should not be allowed.

Ninth Maxim:

Let the wise wife, who cares for her good name,
Decline to play at any gambling game.
In such seductive pastimes wives can lose
Far more than coins, or bills, or I.O.U.'s.

Tenth Maxim:

It is not good for wives
To go on gay excursions,
Picnics, or country drives.

75

In all such light diversions,
No matter who's the host,
The husbands pay the most.

Eleventh Maxim—

ARNOLPHE

Good. Read the rest to yourself. I'll clarify
Whatever may confuse you, by and by.
I've just recalled some business I'd forgot;
'T will only take a moment, like as not.
Go in, and treat that precious book with care.
If the notary comes, tell him to have a chair.

SCENE THREE

ARNOLPHE

ARNOLPHE

What could be safer than to marry her?
She'll do and be whatever I prefer.
She's like a lump of wax, and I can mold her
Into what shape I like, as she grows older.
True, she was almost lured away from me,
Whilst I was gone, through her simplicity;
But if one's wife must have some imperfection,
It's best that she should err in that direction.
Such faults as hers are easy to remove:
A simple wife is eager to improve,
And if she has been led astray, a slight
Admonitory talk will set her right.
But a clever wife's another kettle of fish:
One's at the mercy of her every wish;
What she desires, she'll have at any cost,
And reasoning with her is labor lost.
Her wicked wit makes virtues of her crimes,
Makes mock of principle, and oftentimes
Contrives, in furtherance of some wicked plan,
Intrigues which can defeat the shrewdest man.
Against her there is no defense, for she's
Unbeatable at plots and strategies,
And once she has resolved to amputate
Her husband's honor, he must bow to fate.

77

There's many a decent man could tell that story.
But that young fool will have no chance to glory
In my disgrace: he has too loose a tongue,
And that's a fault of Frenchmen, old or young.
When they are lucky in a love affair,
To keep the secret's more than they can bear;
A foolish vanity torments them, till
They'd rather hang, by Heaven, than be still.
What but the spells of Satan could incline
Women to favor men so asinine?
But here he comes; my feelings must not show
As I extract from him his tale of woe.

SCENE FOUR

HORACE, ARNOLPHE

HORACE

I've just been at your house, and I begin
To fear I'm fated never to find you in.
But I'll persist, and one day have the joy—

ARNOLPHE

Ah, come, no idle compliments, my boy.
All this fine talk, so flowery and so polished,
Is something I'd be glad to see abolished.
It's a vile custom: most men waste two-thirds
Of every day exchanging empty words.
Let's put our hats on, now, and be at ease.
Well, how's your love life going? Do tell me, please.
I was a bit distrait when last we met,
But what you told me I did not forget:
Your bold beginnings left me much impressed,
And now I'm all agog to hear the rest.

HORACE

Since I unlocked my heart to you, alas,
My hopes have come to an unhappy pass.

[*Act Three · Scene Four*]

ARNOLPHE

Oh, dear! How so?

HORACE

       Just now—alas—I learned
That my beloved's guardian has returned.

ARNOLPHE

That's bad.

HORACE

       What's more, he's well aware that we've
Been meeting secretly, without his leave.

ARNOLPHE

But how could he so quickly find that out?

HORACE

I don't know, but he has, beyond a doubt.
I went at my usual hour, more or less,
To pay my homage to her loveliness,
And found the servants changed in attitude.
They barred my way; their words and looks were rude.
"Be off!" they told me, and with no good grace
They slammed the door directly in my face.

ARNOLPHE

Right in your face!

HORACE

Yes.

ARNOLPHE

Dreadful. Tell me more.

HORACE

I tried to reason with them through the door,
But whatsoever I said to them, they cried,
"The master says you're not to come inside."

ARNOLPHE

They wouldn't open it?

HORACE

No. And then Agnès,
On orders from her guardian, as one could guess,
Came to her window, said that she was sick
Of my attentions, and threw down a brick.

ARNOLPHE

A brick, you say!

HORACE

A brick; and it wasn't small.
Not what one hopes for when one pays a call.

[*Act Three · Scene Four*]

ARNOLPHE

Confound it! That's no mild rebuff, my lad.
I fear your situation's pretty bad.

HORACE

Yes, that old fool's return has spoiled my game.

ARNOLPHE

You have my deepest sympathy; it's a shame.

HORACE

He's wrecked my plans.

ARNOLPHE

          Oh, come; you've lost some
                ground,
But some means of recouping will be found.

HORACE

With a little inside help, I might by chance
Outwit this jealous fellow's vigilance.

ARNOLPHE

That should be easy. The lady, as you say,
Loves you.

[*Act Three · Scene Four*]

HORACE

Indeed, yes.

ARNOLPHE

Then you'll find a way.

HORACE

I hope so.

ARNOLPHE

You must not be put to flight
By that ungracious brick.

HORACE

Of course you're right.
I knew at once that that old fool was back
And secretly directing the attack.
But what amazed me (you'll be amazed as well)
Was something else she did, of which I'll tell—
A daring trick one wouldn't expect to see
Played by a girl of such simplicity.
Love is indeed a wondrous master, Sir,
Whose teaching makes us what we never were,
And under whose miraculous tuition
One suddenly can change one's disposition.
It overturns our settled inclinations,
Causing the most astounding transformations:
The miser's made a spendthrift overnight,
The coward valiant, and the boor polite;

Love spurs the sluggard on to high endeavor,
And moves the artless maiden to be clever.
Well, such a miracle has changed Agnès.
She cried, just now, with seeming bitterness,
"Go! I refuse to see you, and don't ask why;
To all your questions, here is my reply!"—
And having made that statement, down she threw
The brick I've mentioned, and a letter, too.
Note how her words apply to brick *and* letter:
Isn't that fine? Could any ruse be better?
Aren't you amazed? Do you see what great effect
True love can have upon the intellect?
Can you deny its power to inspire
The gentlest heart with fortitude and fire?
How do you like that trick with the letter, eh?
A most astute young woman, wouldn't you say?
As for my jealous rival, isn't the role
He's played in this affair extremely droll?
Well?

ARNOLPHE

Yes, quite droll.

HORACE

                    Well, laugh, if that's the case!
(*Arnolphe gives a forced laugh.*)
My, what a fool! He fortifies his place
Against me, using bricks for cannon balls,
As if he feared that I might storm the walls;
What's more, in his anxiety he rallies
His two domestics to repulse my sallies;
And then he's hoodwinked by the girl he meant

84

To keep forever meek and innocent!
I must confess that, though this silly man's
Return to town has balked my amorous plans,
The whole thing's been so comical that I find
That I'm convulsed whenever it comes to mind.
You haven't laughed as much as I thought you would.

ARNOLPHE, with a forced laugh

I beg your pardon; I've done the best I could.

HORACE

But let me show you the letter she wrote, my friend.
What her heart feels, her artless hand has penned
In the most touching terms, the sweetest way,
With pure affection, purest naïveté;
Nature herself, I think, would so express
Love's first awakening and its sweet distress.

ARNOLPHE, aside

Behold what scribbling leads to! It was quite
Against my wishes that she learned to write.

HORACE, reading

I am moved to write to you, but I am much at a loss
as to how to begin. I have thoughts which I should like
you to know of; but I don't know how to go about telling
them to you, and I mistrust my own words. I begin to
perceive that I have always been kept in a state of ig-
norance, and so I am fearful of writing something I
shouldn't, or of saying more than I ought. In truth, I

don't know what you have done to me, but I know that
I am mortally vexed by the harsh things I am made to do
to you, that it will be the most painful thing in the world
to give you up, and that I would be happy indeed to be
yours. Perhaps it is rash of me to say that; but in any case
I cannot help saying it, and I wish that I could have my
desire without doing anything wrong. I am constantly
told that all young men are deceivers, that they mustn't
be listened to, and that all you have said to me is mere
trickery; I assure you, however, that I have not yet been
able to think that of you, and your words so touch me
that I cannot believe them false. Please tell me frankly
what you intend; for truly, since my own intentions are
blameless, it would be very wicked of you to deceive me,
and I think that I should die of despair.

ARNOLPHE, *aside*

The bitch!

HORACE

What's wrong?

ARNOLPHE

Oh, nothing: I was sneezing.

HORACE

Was ever a style so amiable, so pleasing?
Despite the tyranny she's had to bear,
Isn't her nature sweet beyond compare?
And is it not a crime of the basest kind

For anyone to stifle such a mind,
To starve so fine a spirit, and to enshroud
In ignorance a soul so well-endowed?
Love has begun to waken her, however,
And if some kind star favors my endeavor
I'll free her from that utter beast, that black
Villain, that wretch, that brute, that maniac—

ARNOLPHE

Good-bye.

HORACE

What, going?

ARNOLPHE

I've just recalled that I'm
Due somewhere else in a few minutes' time.

HORACE

Wait! Can you think of someone who might possess
An entrée to that house, and to Agnès?
I hate to trouble you, but do please lend
Whatever help you can, as friend to friend.
The servants, as I said, both man and maid,
Have turned against my cause, and can't be swayed.
Just now, despite my every blandishment,
They eyed me coldly, and would not relent.
I had, for a time, the aid of an old woman
Whose talent for intrigue was superhuman;
She served me, at the start, with much success,

87

But died four days ago, to my distress.
Don't you know someone who could help me out?

ARNOLPHE

I don't; but you'll find someone, I don't doubt.

HORACE

Farewell, then, Sir. You'll be discreet, I know.

SCENE FIVE

ARNOLPHE

ARNOLPHE

In that boy's presence, what hell I undergo,
Trying to hide my anguish from his eye!
To think that an innocent girl should prove so sly!
Either she's fooled me, and never *was* naïve,
Or Satan's just now taught her to deceive.
That cursèd letter! I wish that I were dead.
Plainly that callow wretch has turned her head,
Captured her mind and heart, eclipsed me there,
And doomed me to distraction and despair.
The loss of her entails a double hell:
My honor suffers, and my love as well.
It drives me mad to see myself displaced,
And all my careful planning gone to waste.
To be revenged on her, I need but wait
And let her giddy passion meet its fate;
The upshot can't be anything but bad.
But oh, to lose the thing one loves is sad.
Good Lord! To rear her with such calculation,
And then fall victim to infatuation!
She has no funds, no family, yet she can dare
Abuse my lavish kindness and my care;
And what, for Heaven's sake, is my reaction?
In spite of all, I love her to distraction!
Have you no shame, fool? Don't you resent her crimes?

89

Oh, I could slap my face a thousand times!
I'll go inside for a bit, but only to see
How she will face me after her treachery.
Kind Heaven, let no dishonor stain my brow;
Or if it is decreed that I must bow
To that misfortune, lend me at least, I pray,
Such patient strength as some poor men display.

ACT 4

SCENE ONE

ARNOLPHE, *entering from the house, alone*

I can't hold still a minute, I declare.
My anxious thoughts keep darting here and there,
Planning defenses, seeking to prevent
That rascal from achieving his intent.
How calm the traitress looked when I went in!
Despite her crimes, she shows no sense of sin,
And though she's all but sent me to my grave,
How like a little saint she dares behave!
The more she sat there, cool and unperturbed,
The less I thought my fury could be curbed;
Yet, strange to say, my heart's increasing ire
Seemed only to redouble my desire.
I was embittered, desperate, irate,
And yet her beauty had never seemed so great.
Never did her bright eyes so penetrate me,
So rouse my spirit, so infatuate me;
Oh, it would break the heart within my breast
Should fate subject me to this cruel jest.
What! Have I supervised her education
With loving care and long consideration,
Sheltered her since she was a tiny creature,
Cherished sweet expectations for her future,
For thirteen years molded her character
And based my hopes of happiness on her,

93

Only to see some young fool steal the prize
Of her affection, under my very eyes,
And just when she and I were all but wed?
Ah, no, young friend! Ah, no, young chucklehead!
I mean to stop you; I swear that you shall not
Succeed, however well you scheme and plot,
And that you'll have no cause to laugh at me.

SCENE TWO

NOTARY

Ah, here you are, Sir! I am the notary.
So, there's a contract which you'd have me draw?

ARNOLPHE, *unaware of the notary*

How shall I do it?

NOTARY

According to the law.

ARNOLPHE, *still oblivious*

I must be prudent, and think what course is best.

NOTARY

I shall do nothing against your interest.

ARNOLPHE, *oblivious*

One must anticipate the unexpected.

[*Act Four · Scene Two*]

NOTARY

In my hands, you'll be thoroughly protected.
But do remember, lest you be betrayed,
To sign no contract till the dowry's paid.

ARNOLPHE, *oblivious*

I must act covertly; if this thing gets out,
The gossips will have much to blab about.

NOTARY

If you're so anxious not to make a stir,
The contract can be drawn in secret, Sir.

ARNOLPHE, *oblivious*

But how shall she be dealt with? Can I condone—

NOTARY

The dowry is proportional to her own.

ARNOLPHE, *oblivious*

It's hard to be strict with one whom you adore.

NOTARY

In that case, you may wish to give her more.

ARNOLPHE, *oblivious*

How should I treat the girl? I must decide.

[*Act Four · Scene Two*]

NOTARY

As a general rule, the husband gives the bride
A dowry that's one-third the size of hers;
But he may increase the sum, if he prefers.

ARNOLPHE, *oblivious*

If—

NOTARY, *Arnolphe now noticing him*

As for property, and its division
In case of death, the husband makes provision
As he thinks best.

ARNOLPHE

Eh?

NOTARY

He can make certain of
His bride's security, and show his love,
By jointure, or a settlement whereby
The gift is canceled should the lady die,
Reverting to her heirs, if so agreed;
Or go by common law; or have a deed
Of gift appended to the instrument,
Either by his sole wish, or by consent.
Why shrug your shoulders? Am I talking rot?
Do I know contracts, Sir, or do I not?
Who could instruct me? Who would be so bold?
Do I not know that spouses jointly hold

97

Goods, chattels, lands, and money in their two names,
Unless one party should renounce all claims?
Do I not know that a third of the bride's resources
Enters the joint estate—

ARNOLPHE

All that, of course, is
True. But who asked for all this pedantry?

NOTARY

You did! And now you sniff and shrug at me,
And treat my competence with ridicule.

ARNOLPHE

The devil take this ugly-featured fool!
Good day, good day. An end to all this chatter.

NOTARY

Did you not ask my aid in a legal matter?

ARNOLPHE

Yes, yes, but now the matter's been deferred.
When your advice is needed, I'll send word.
Meanwhile, stop blathering, you blatherskite!

NOTARY

He's mad, I judge; and I think my judgment's right.

SCENE THREE

NOTARY, *to Alain and Georgette*

Your master sent you to fetch me, isn't that so?

ALAIN

Yes.

NOTARY

How you feel about him I don't know,
But I regard him as a senseless boor.
Tell him I said so.

GEORGETTE

We will, you may be sure.

SCENE FOUR

ALAIN, GEORGETTE, ARNOLPHE

ALAIN

Sir—

ARNOLPHE

 Ah, come here, my good friends, tried and true:
You've amply proved that I may count on you.

ALAIN

The notary—

ARNOLPHE

 Tell me later, will you not?
My honor's threatened by a vicious plot;
Think, children, what distress you'd feel, what shame,
If some dishonor touched your master's name!
You wouldn't dare to leave the house, for fear
That all the town would point at you, and sneer.
Since we're together, then, in this affair,
You must be ever watchful, and take care
That no approach that gallant may adopt—

[*Act Four · Scene Four*]

GEORGETTE

We've learned our lesson, Sir; he shall be stopped.

ARNOLPHE

Beware his fine words and his flatteries.

ALAIN

Of course.

GEORGETTE

We can resist such talk with ease.

ARNOLPHE, *to Alain*

What if he said, "Alain, for mercy's sake,
Do me a kindness"—what answer would you make?

ALAIN

I'd say, "You fool!"

ARNOLPHE

Good, good. (*To Georgette:*)
"Georgette, my dear,
I'm sure you're just as sweet as you appear."

GEORGETTE

"Fathead!"

[*Act Four · Scene Four*]

ARNOLPHE

Good, good. (*To Alain:*) "Come, let me in.
You know
That my intent is pure as the driven snow."

ALAIN

"Sir, you're a knave!"

ARNOLPHE

Well said. (*To Georgette:*) "Un-
less you take
Pity on my poor heart, it's sure to break."

GEORGETTE

"You are an impudent ass!"

ARNOLPHE

Well said, Georgette.
"I'm not the sort of person to forget
A favor, or begrudge the *quid pro quo,*
As these few coins, Alain, will serve to show.
And you, Georgette, take this and buy a dress.
      (*Both hold out their hands and take the money.*)
That's but a specimen of my largesse.
And all I ask is that you grant to me
An hour of your young mistress' company."

GEORGETTE, *giving him a shove*

"You're crazy!"

[*Act Four · Scene Four*]

ARNOLPHE

Good!

ALAIN, *shoving Arnolphe*

"Move on!"

ARNOLPHE

Good!

GEORGETTE, *shoving Arnolphe*

"Out of my
sight!"

ARNOLPHE

Good, good—but that's enough.

GEORGETTE

Did I do it right?

ALAIN

Is that how we're to treat him?

ARNOLPHE

You were fine;
Except for the money, which you should decline.

[*Act Four · Scene Four*]

GEORGETTE

We didn't think, Sir. That was wrong indeed.

ALAIN

Would you like to do it over again?

ARNOLPHE

                                   No need;
Go back inside.

ALAIN

            Sir, if you say the word, we—

ARNOLPHE

No, that will do; go in at once; you heard me.
Just keep the money; I shall be with you shortly.
Be on your guard, and ready to support me.

SCENE FIVE

ARNOLPHE

ARNOLPHE

The cobbler at the corner is sharp of eye;
I think that I'll enlist him as a spy.
As for Agnès, I'll keep her under guard,
And all dishonest women shall be barred—
Hairdressers, glovers, handkerchief-makers, those
Who come to the door with ribbons, pins, and bows,
And often, as a sideline to such wares,
Are go-betweens in secret love affairs.
I know the world, and the tricks that people use;
That boy will have to invent some brand-new ruse
If he's to get a message in to her.

SCENE SIX

HORACE, ARNOLPHE

HORACE

What luck to find you in this quarter, Sir!
I've just had a narrow escape, believe you me!
Just after I left you, whom did I chance to see
Upon her shady balcony, but the fair
Agnès, who had come out to take the air!
She managed, having signaled me to wait,
To steal downstairs and open the garden gate.
We went to her room, and were no sooner there
Than we heard her jealous guardian on the stair;
In which great peril I was thrust by her
Into a wardrobe where her dresses were.
He entered. I couldn't see him, but I heard
Him striding back and forth without a word,
Heaving deep sighs of woe again and again,
Pounding upon the tables now and then,
Kicking a little dog, who yipped in fright,
And throwing her possessions left and right.
What's more, to give his fury full release,
He knocked two vases off her mantelpiece.
Clearly the old goat had some vague, dismaying
Sense of the tricks his captive had been playing.
At last, when all his anger had been spent
On objects which were dumb and innocent,
The frantic man, without a word, went striding

Out of the room, and I came out of hiding.
Quite naturally, we didn't dare extend
Our rendezvous, because our jealous friend
Was still about; tonight, however, I
Shall visit her, quite late, and on the sly.
Our plan is this: I'll cough, three times, outside;
At that, the window will be opened wide;
Then, with a ladder and the assistance of
Agnès, I'll climb into our bower of love.
Since you're my only friend, I tell you this—
For telling, as you know, augments one's bliss.
However vast the joy, one must confide
In someone else before one's satisfied.
You share, I know, my happy expectations.
But now, farewell; I must make preparations.

SCENE SEVEN

ARNOLPHE

ARNOLPHE

The evil star that's hounding me to death
Gives me no time in which to catch my breath!
Must I, again and again, be forced to see
My measures foiled through their complicity?
Shall I, at my ripe age, be duped, forsooth,
By a green girl and by a harebrained youth?
For twenty years I've sagely contemplated
The woeful lives of men unwisely mated,
And analyzed with care the slips whereby
The best-planned marriages have gone awry;
Thus schooled by others' failures, I felt that I'd
Be able, when I chose to take a bride,
To ward off all mischance, and be protected
From griefs to which so many are subjected.
I took, to that end, all the shrewd and wise
Precautions which experience could devise;
Yet, as if fate had made the stern decision
That no man living should escape derision,
I find, for all my pondering of this
Great matter, all my keen analysis,
The twenty years and more which I have spent
In planning to escape the embarrassment
So many husbands suffer from today,
That I'm as badly victimized as they.

But no, damned fate, I challenge your decree!
The lovely prize is in my custody,
And though her heart's been filched by that young pest,
I guarantee that he'll not get the rest,
And that this evening's gallant rendezvous
Won't go as smoothly as they'd like it to.
There's one good thing about my present fix—
That I'm forewarned of all my rival's tricks,
And that this oaf who's aiming to undo me
Confesses all his bad intentions to me.

SCENE EIGHT

CHRYSALDE, ARNOLPHE

CHRYSALDE

Well, shall we dine, and then go out for a stroll?

ARNOLPHE

No, no, the dinner's off.

CHRYSALDE

Well, well, how droll!

ARNOLPHE

Forgive me: there's a crisis I must face.

CHRYSALDE

Your wedding plans have changed? Is that the case?

ARNOLPHE

I have no need of your solicitude.

[*Act Four · Scene Eight*]

CHRYSALDE

Tell me your troubles, now, and don't be rude.
I'd guess, friend, that your marriage scheme has met
With difficulties, and that you're upset.
To judge by your expression, I'd almost swear it.

ARNOLPHE

Whatever happens, I shall have the merit
Of not resembling some in this community,
Who let young gallants cheat them with impunity.

CHRYSALDE

It's odd that you, with your good intellect,
Are so obsessive in this one respect,
Measure all happiness thereby, and base
On it alone men's honor or disgrace.
Greed, envy, vice, and cowardice are not
Important sins to you; the one grave blot
You find on any scutcheon seems to be
The crime of having suffered cuckoldry.
Now, come: shall a man be robbed of his good name
Through an ill chance for which he's not to blame?
Shall a good husband lacerate his soul
With guilt for matters not in his control?
When a man marries, why must we scorn or praise him
According to whether or not his wife betrays him?
And if she does so, why must her husband see
The fact as an immense catastrophe?
Do realize that, to a man of sense,
There's nothing crushing in such accidents;
That, since no man can dodge the blows of fate,

One's sense of failure should not be too great,
And that there's no harm done, whatever they say,
If one but takes things in the proper way.
In difficulties of this sort, it seems,
As always, wiser to avoid extremes.
One shouldn't ape those husbands who permit
Such scandal, and who take a pride in it,
Dropping the names of their wives' latest gallants,
Praising their persons, bragging of their talents,
Professing warm regard for them, attending
The parties that they give, and so offending
Society, which properly resents
Displays of laxity and impudence.
Needless to say, such conduct will not do;
And yet the other extreme's improper too.
If men do wrong to flatter their wives' gallants,
It's no less bad when, lacking tact and balance,
They vent their grievances with savage fury,
Calling the whole world to be judge and jury,
And won't be satisfied till they acquaint
All ears whatever with their loud complaint.
Between these two extremes, my friend, there lies
A middle way that's favored by the wise,
And which, if followed, will preserve one's face
However much one's wife may court disgrace.
In short, then, cuckoldry need not be dreaded
Like some dire monster, fierce and many-headed;
It can be lived with, if one has the wit
To take it calmly, and make the best of it.

ARNOLPHE

For that fine speech, the great fraternity
Of cuckolds owes you thanks, your Excellency;

And all men, if they heard your wisdom, would
Make joyous haste to join the brotherhood.

CHRYSALDE

No, that I shouldn't approve. But since it's fate
Whereby we're joined to one or another mate,
One should take marriage as one takes picquette,
In which, if one has made a losing bet,
One takes the setback calmly, and takes pains
To do the best one can with what remains.

ARNOLPHE

In other words, eat hearty and sleep tight,
And tell yourself that everything's all right.

CHRYSALDE

Laugh on, my friend; but I can, in all sobriety,
Name fifty things which cause me more anxiety,
And would, if they occurred, appall me more
Than this misfortune which you so abhor.
Had I to choose between adversities,
I'd rather be a cuckold, if you please,
Than marry one of those good wives who find
Continual reason to upbraid mankind,
Those virtuous shrews, those fiendish paragons,
As violently chaste as Amazons,
Who, having had the goodness not to horn us,
Accord themselves the right to nag and scorn us,
And make us pay for their fidelity
By being as vexatious as can be.
Do learn, friend, that when all is said and done,

Cuckoldry's what you make of it; that one
Might welcome it in certain situations,
And that, like all things, it has compensations.

ARNOLPHE

Well, if you want it, may you get your wish;
But, as for me, it's not at all my dish.
Before I'd let my brow be decked with horn—

CHRYSALDE

Tut, tut! Don't swear, or you may be forsworn.
If fate has willed it, your resolves will fail,
And all your oaths will be of no avail.

ARNOLPHE

I! I a cuckold?

CHRYSALDE

        Don't let it fret you so.
It happens to the best of men, you know.
Cuckolds exist with whom, if I may be frank,
You can't compare for person, wealth, or rank.

ARNOLPHE

I have no wish to be compared with such.
Enough, now, of your mockery; it's too much.
You try my patience.

[*Act Four · Scene Eight*]

CHRYSALDE

          So, you're annoyed with me?
Ah, well. Good-bye. But bear in mind that he
Who thumps his chest and swears upon his soul
That he will never play the cuckold's role
Is studying for the part, and may well get it.

ARNOLPHE

That won't occur, I swear; I shall not let it.
I shall remove that threat this very minute.
         (*He knocks at his own gate.*)

SCENE NINE

ARNOLPHE

My friends, the battle's joined, and we must win it.
Your love for me, by which I'm touched and moved,
Must now, in this emergency, be proved,
And if your deeds repay my confidence,
You may expect a handsome recompense.
This very night—don't tell a soul, my friends—
A certain rascal whom you know intends
To scale the wall and see Agnès; but we
Shall lay a little trap for him, we three.
You'll both be armed with clubs, and when the young
Villain has almost reached the topmost rung
(I meanwhile shall have flung the shutters wide),
You shall lean out and so lambaste his hide,
So bruise his ribs by your combined attack,
That he will never dream of coming back.
Don't speak my name while this is happening, mind you,
Or let him know that I am there behind you.
Have you the pluck to serve me in this action?

ALAIN

If blows are called for, we can give satisfaction.
I'll show you that this good right arm's not lame.

GEORGETTE

Mine looks less strong than his, but all the same
Our foe will know that he's been beaten by it.

ARNOLPHE

Go in, then; and, whatever you do, keep quiet.
                    (*Alone:*)
Tonight, I'll give a lesson to mankind.
If all endangered husbands took a mind
To greet their wives' intrusive gallants thus,
Cuckolds, I think, would be less numerous.

ACT 5

SCENE ONE

ARNOLPHE

You brutes! What made you be so heavy-handed?

ALAIN

But, Sir, we only did as you commanded.

ARNOLPHE

Don't put the blame on me; your guilt is plain.
I wished him beaten; I didn't wish him slain.
And furthermore, if you'll recall, I said
To hit him on the ribs, not on the head.
It's a ghastly situation in which I'm placed;
How is this young man's murder to be faced?
Go in, now, and be silent as the grave
About that innocent command I gave.
                    (*Alone:*)
It's nearly daybreak. I must take thought, and see
How best to cope with this dire tragedy.
God help me! What will the boy's father say
When this appalling story comes his way?

SCENE TWO

HORACE, ARNOLPHE

HORACE

Who's this, I wonder. I'd best approach with care.

ARNOLPHE

How could I have foreseen . . . I say, who's there?

HORACE

Seigneur Arnolphe?

ARNOLPHE

Yes—

HORACE

It's Horace, once more.
My, you're up early! I was heading for
Your house, to ask a favor.

ARNOLPHE

Oh, God, I'm dizzy.
Is he a vision? Is he a ghost? What is he?

122

HORACE

Sir, I'm in trouble once again, I fear.
It's providential that you should appear
Just at the moment when your help was needed.
My plans, I'm happy to tell you, have succeeded
Beyond all expectations, and despite
An incident which might have spoiled them quite.
I don't know how it happened, but someone knew
About our contemplated rendezvous;
For, just as I'd almost reached her window sill,
I saw some frightful figures, armed to kill,
Lean out above me, waving their clubs around.
I lost my footing, tumbled to the ground,
And thus, though rather scratched and bruised, was spared
The thumping welcome which they had prepared.
Those brutes (of whom Old Jealous, I suppose,
Was one) ascribed my tumble to their blows,
And since I lay there, motionless, in the dirt
For several minutes, being stunned and hurt,
They judged that they had killed me, and they all
Took fright at that, and so began to brawl.
I lay in silence, hearing their angry cries:
They blamed each other for my sad demise,
Then tiptoed out, in darkness and in dread,
To feel my body, and see if I were dead.
As you can well imagine, I played the part
Of a limp, broken corpse with all my heart.
Quite overcome with terror, they withdrew,
And I was thinking of withdrawing, too,
When young Agnès came hurrying, out of breath
And much dismayed by my supposèd death:
She had been able, of course, to overhear
All that my foes had babbled in their fear,

And while they were distracted and unnerved
She'd slipped from the house, entirely unobserved.
Ah, how she wept with happiness when she found
That I was, after all, both safe and sound!
Well, to be brief: electing to be guided
*By her own heart, the charming girl decided
Not to return to her guardian, but to flee,
Entrusting her security to me.
What must his tyranny be, if it can force
So shy a girl to take so bold a course!
And think what peril she might thus incur,
If I were capable of wronging her.
Ah, but my love's too pure for that, too strong;
I'd rather die than do her any wrong;
So admirable is she that all I crave
Is to be with her even to the grave.
I know my father: this will much displease him,
But we shall manage somehow to appease him.
In any case, she's won my heart, and I
Could not desert her, even if I chose to try.
The favor I ask of you is rather large:
It's that you take my darling in your charge,
And keep her, if you will, for several days
In your own house, concealed from the world's gaze.
I ask your help in this because I'm bent
On throwing all pursuers off the scent;
Also because, if she were seen with me,
There might be talk of impropriety.
To you, my loyal friend, I've dared to impart,
Without reserve, the secrets of my heart,
And likewise it's to you I now confide
My dearest treasure and my future bride.

[*Act Five · Scene Two*]

ARNOLPHE

I'm at your service; on that you may depend.

HORACE

You'll grant the favor that I ask, dear friend?

ARNOLPHE

Of course; most willingly. I'm glad indeed
That I can help you in your hour of need.
Thank Heaven that you asked me! There's no request
To which I could accede with greater zest.

HORACE

How kind you are! What gratitude I feel!
I feared you might refuse my rash appeal;
But you're a man of the world, urbane and wise,
Who looks upon young love with tolerant eyes.
My man is guarding her, just down the street.

ARNOLPHE

It's almost daylight. Where had we better meet?
Someone might see me, if you brought her here,
And should you bring her to my house, I fear
'T would start the servants talking. We must look
For some more shadowy and secluded nook.
That garden's handy; I shall await her there.

[*Act Five* · *Scene Two*]

HORACE

You're right, Sir. We must act with the utmost care.
I'll go, and quickly bring Agnès to you,
Then seek my lodgings without more ado.

ARNOLPHE, *alone*

Ah, Fortune! This good turn will compensate
For all the tricks you've played on me of late.
                    (*He hides his face in his cloak.*)

SCENE THREE

HORACE

Just come with me; there's no cause for alarm.
I'm taking you where you'll be safe from harm.
To stay together would be suicide:
Go in, and let this gentleman be your guide.
    (*Arnolphe, whom she does not recognize,
    takes her hand.*)

AGNÈS

Why are you leaving me?

HORACE

            Dear Agnès, I must.

AGNÈS

You'll very soon be coming back, I trust?

HORACE

I shall; my yearning heart will see to that.

[*Act Five · Scene Three*]

AGNÈS

Without you, life is miserable and flat.

HORACE

When I'm away from you, I pine and grieve.

AGNÈS

Alas! If that were so, you wouldn't leave.

HORACE

You know how strong my love is, and how true.

AGNÈS

Ah, no, you don't love me as I love you.
    (*Arnolphe tugs at her hand.*)
Why does he pull my hand?

HORACE

            'T would ruin us,
My dear, if we were seen together thus,
And therefore this true friend, who's filled with worry
About our welfare, urges you to hurry.

AGNÈS

But why must I go with him—a perfect stranger?

[*Act Five · Scene Three*]

HORACE

Don't fret. In his hands you'll be out of danger.

AGNÈS

I'd rather be in *your* hands; that was why—
     (*To Arnolphe, who tugs her hand again:*)
Wait, wait.

HORACE

It's daybreak. I must go. Good-bye.

AGNÈS

When shall I see you?

HORACE

Very soon, I swear.

AGNÈS

Till that sweet moment, I'll be in despair.

HORACE, *leaving, to himself*

My happiness is assured; my fears may cease;
Praise be to Heaven, I now can sleep in peace.

SCENE FOUR

ARNOLPHE, *hiding his face in his cloak, and*
disguising his voice

Come, this is not where you're to stay, my child;
It's elsewhere that you shall be domiciled.
You're going to a safe, sequestered place.
  (*Revealing himself, and using his normal voice:*)
Do you know me?

AGNÈS, *recognizing him*

  Aagh!

ARNOLPHE

      You wicked girl! My face
Would seem, just now, to give you rather a fright.
Oh, clearly I'm a most unwelcome sight:
I interfere with your romantic plan.
  (*Agnès turns and looks in vain for Horace.*)
No use to look for help from that young man;
He couldn't hear you now; he's gone too far.
Well, well! For one so young, how sly you are!
You ask—most innocently, it would appear—
If children are begotten through the ear,
Yet you know all too well, I now discover,

130

How to keep trysts—at midnight—with a lover!
What honeyed words you spoke to him just now!
Who taught you such beguilements? Tell me how,
Within so short a time, you've learned so much!
You used to be afraid of ghosts and such:
Has your gallant taught you not to fear the night?
You ingrate! To deceive me so, despite
The loving care with which you have been blessed!
Oh, I have warmed a serpent at my breast
Until, reviving, it unkindly bit
The very hand that was caressing it!

AGNÈS

Why are you cross with me?

ARNOLPHE

Oh! So I'm unfair?

AGNÈS

I've done no wrong of which I am aware.

ARNOLPHE

Was it right, then, to run off with that young beau?

AGNÈS

He wants me for his wife; he's told me so.
I've only done as you advised; you said
That, so as not to sin, one ought to wed.

ARNOLPHE

Yes, but I made it perfectly clear that I'd
Resolved, myself, to take you as my bride.

AGNÈS

Yes; but if I may give my point of view,
He'd suit me, as a husband, better than you.
In all your talk of marriage, you depict
A state that's gloomy, burdensome, and strict;
But, ah! when *he* describes the married state,
It sounds so sweet that I can hardly wait.

ARNOLPHE

Ah! So you love him, faithless girl!

AGNÈS

Why, yes.

ARNOLPHE

Have you the gall to tell me that, Agnès?

AGNÈS

If it's the truth, what's wrong with telling it?

ARNOLPHE

How dared you fall in love with him, you chit?

AGNÈS

It was no fault of mine; he made me do it.
I was in love with him before I knew it.

ARNOLPHE

You should have overcome your amorous feeling.

AGNÈS

It's hard to overcome what's so appealing.

ARNOLPHE

Didn't you know that I would be put out?

AGNÈS

Why, no. What have you to complain about?

ARNOLPHE

Nothing, of course! I'm wild with happiness!
You don't, I take it, love me.

AGNÈS

Love you?

ARNOLPHE

Yes.

[*Act Five · Scene Four*]

AGNÈS

Alas, I don't.

ARNOLPHE

You *don't?*

AGNÈS

Would you have me lie?

ARNOLPHE

Why don't you love me, hussy? Tell me why!

AGNÈS

Good heavens, it's not I whom you should blame.
He made me love him; why didn't you do the same?
I didn't hinder you, as I recall.

ARNOLPHE

I tried to make you love me; I gave my all;
Yet all my pains and strivings were in vain.

AGNÈS

He has more aptitude than you, that's plain;
To win my heart, he scarcely had to try.

[*Act Five · Scene Four*]

ARNOLPHE, *aside*

This peasant girl can frame a neat reply!
What lady wit could answer with more art?
Either she's bright, or in what concerns the heart
A foolish girl can best the wisest man.
    (*To Agnès:*)
Well, then, Miss Back-Talk, answer this if you can:
Did I raise you, all these years, at such expense,
For another's benefit? Does that make sense?

AGNÈS

No. But he'll gladly pay you for your trouble.

ARNOLPHE, *aside*

Such flippancy! It makes my rage redouble.
    (*To Agnès:*)
You minx! How could he possibly discharge
Your obligations to me? They're too large.

AGNÈS

Frankly, they don't seem very large to me.

ARNOLPHE

Did I not nurture you from infancy?

AGNÈS

Yes, that you did. I'm deeply obligated.
How wondrously you've had me educated!

Do you fancy that I'm blind to what you've done,
And cannot see that I'm a simpleton?
Oh, it humiliates me; I revolt
Against the shame of being such a dolt.

ARNOLPHE

Do you think you'll gain the knowledge that you need
Through that young dandy's tutelage?

AGNÈS

                              Yes, indeed.
It's thanks to him I know what little I do;
I owe far more to him than I do to you.

ARNOLPHE

What holds me back, I ask myself, from treating
So insolent a girl to a sound beating?
Your coldness irks me to the point of tears,
And it would ease my soul to box your ears.

AGNÈS

Alas, then, beat me, if you so desire.

ARNOLPHE, *aside*

Those words and that sweet look dissolve my ire,
Restoring to my heart such tender feeling
As makes me quite forget her double-dealing.
How strange love is! How strange that men, from such
Perfidious beings, will endure so much!

Women, as all men know, are frailly wrought:
They're foolish and illogical in thought,
Their souls are weak, their characters are bad,
There's nothing quite so silly, quite so mad,
So faithless; yet, despite these sorry features,
What won't we do to please the wretched creatures?
     (*To Agnès:*)
Come, traitress, let us be at peace once more.
I'll pardon you, and love you as before.
Repay my magnanimity, and learn
From my great love to love me in return.

                AGNÈS

Truly, if I were able to, I would.
I'd gladly love you if I only could.

             ARNOLPHE

You can, my little beauty, if you'll but try.
     (*He sighs.*)
Just listen to that deep and yearning sigh!
Look at my haggard face! See how it suffers!
Reject that puppy, and the love he offers:
He must have cast a spell on you; with me,
You'll be far happier, I guarantee.
I know that clothes and jewels are your passion;
Don't worry: you shall always be in fashion.
I'll pet you night and day; you shall be showered
With kisses; you'll be hugged, caressed, devoured.
And you shall have your wish in every way.
I'll say no more; what further could I say?
     (*Aside:*)
Lord, what extremes desire will drive us to!

[*Act Five · Scene Four*]

(*To Agnès:*)

In short, no love could match my love for you.
Tell me, ungrateful girl, what proof do you need?
Shall I weep? Or beat myself until I bleed?
What if I tore my hair out—would that sway you?
Shall I kill myself? Command, and I'll obey you.
I'm ready, cruel one, for you to prove me.

AGNÈS

Somehow, your lengthy speeches fail to move me.
Horace, in two words, could be more engaging.

ARNOLPHE

Enough of this! Your impudence is enraging.
I have my plans for you, you stubborn dunce,
And I shall pack you out of town at once.
You've spurned my love, and baited me as well—
Which you'll repent of in a convent cell.

SCENE FIVE

ALAIN, ARNOLPHE, AGNÈS

ALAIN

It's very strange, but Agnès has vanished, Sir.
I think that corpse has run away with her.

ARNOLPHE

She's here. Go shut her in my room, securely.
That's not where he'd come looking for her, surely,
And she'll be there but half an hour, at most.
Meanwhile I'll get a carriage, in which we'll post
To a safe retreat. Go now, and lock up tight,
And see that you don't let her out of sight.
(*Alone:*)
Perhaps a change of scene and circumstance
Will wean her from this infantile romance.

SCENE SIX

HORACE, ARNOLPHE

HORACE

Seigneur Arnolphe, I'm overwhelmed with grief,
And Heaven's cruelty is beyond belief;
It seems now that a brutal stroke of fate
May force my love and me to separate.
My father, just this minute, chanced to appear,
Alighting from his coach not far from here,
And what has brought him into town this morning
Is a dire errand of which I'd had no warning:
He's made a match for me, and, ready or not,
I am to marry someone on the spot.
Imagine my despair! What blacker curse
Could fall on me, what setback could be worse?
I told you, yesterday, of Enrique. It's he
Who's brought about my present misery;
He's come with Father, to lead me to the slaughter,
And I am doomed to wed his only daughter.
When they told me that, it almost made me swoon;
And, since my father spoke of coming soon
To see you, I excused myself, in fright,
And hastened to forewarn you of my plight.
Take care, Sir, I entreat you, not to let him
Know of Agnès and me; 't would much upset him.
And try, since he so trusts your judgment, to
Dissuade him from the match he has in view.

[*Act Five · Scene Six*]

ARNOLPHE

I shall.

HORACE

That failing, you could be of aid
By urging that the wedding be delayed.

ARNOLPHE

Trust me.

HORACE

On you, my dearest hopes repose.

ARNOLPHE

Fine, fine.

HORACE

You're a father to me, Heaven knows.
Tell him that young men— Ah! He's coming! I spy him.
Here are some arguments with which to ply him.
(*They withdraw to a corner of the stage, and
confer in whispers.*)

SCENE SEVEN

ENRIQUE, ORONTE, CHRYSALDE, HORACE, ARNOLPHE

ENRIQUE, *to Chrysalde*

No need for introductions, Sir. I knew
Your name as soon as I set eyes on you.
You have the very features of your late
Sister, who was my well-belovèd mate;
Oh, how I wish that cruel Destiny
Had let me bring my helpmeet back with me,
After such years of hardship as we bore,
To see her home and family once more.
But fate has ruled that we shall not again
Enjoy her charming presence; let us, then,
Find solace in what joys we may design
For the sole offspring of her love and mine.
You are concerned in this; let us confer,
And see if you approve my plans for her.
Oronte's young son, I think, is a splendid choice;
But in this matter you've an equal voice.

CHRYSALDE

I've better judgment, Brother, than to question
So eminently worthy a suggestion.

[*Act Five · Scene Seven*]

ARNOLPHE, *to Horace*

Yes, yes, don't worry; I'll represent you well.

HORACE

Once more, don't tell him—

ARNOLPHE

     I promise not to tell.
  *(Arnolphe leaves Horace, and crosses to
     embrace Oronte.)*

ORONTE

Ah, my old friend: what a warm, hearty greeting!

ARNOLPHE

Oronte, dear fellow, what a welcome meeting!

ORONTE

I've come to town—

ARNOLPHE

    You needn't say a word;
I know what brings you.

ORONTE

    You've already heard?

[*Act Five · Scene Seven*]

ARNOLPHE

Yes.

ORONTE

Good.

ARNOLPHE

Your son regards this match with dread;
His heart rebels at being forced to wed,
And I've been asked, in fact, to plead his case.
Well, do you know what I'd do, in your place?
I'd exercise a father's rightful sway
And tie the wedding knot without delay.
What the young need, my friend, is discipline;
We only do them harm by giving in.

HORACE, *aside*

Traitor!

CHRYSALDE

If the prospect fills him with revulsion,
Then surely we should not employ compulsion.
My brother-in-law, I trust, would say the same.

ARNOLPHE

Shall a man be governed by his son? For shame!
Would you have a father be so meek and mild
As not to exact obedience from his child?

At his wise age, 't would be grotesque indeed
To see him led by one whom he should lead.
No, no; my dear old friend is honor-bound;
He's given his word, and he must not give ground.
Let him be firm, as a father should, and force
His son to take the necessary course.

ORONTE

Well said: we shall proceed with this alliance,
And I shall answer for my son's compliance.

CHRYSALDE, *to Arnolphe*

It much surprises me to hear you press
For this betrothal with such eagerness.
What is your motive? I can't make you out.

ARNOLPHE

Don't worry, friend; I know what I'm about.

ORONTE

Indeed, Arnolphe—

CHRYSALDE

              He finds that name unpleasant.
Monsieur de la Souche is what he's called at present.

ARNOLPHE

No matter.

[*Act Five · Scene Seven*]

HORACE

What do I hear?

ARNOLPHE, *turning toward Horace*

                Well, now you know,
And now you see why I have spoken so.

HORACE

Oh, what confusion—

SCENE EIGHT

GEORGETTE, ENRIQUE, ORONTE, CHRYSALDE,
HORACE, ARNOLPHE

GEORGETTE

            Sir, please come. Unless
You do, I fear we can't restrain Agnès.
The girl is frantic to escape, I swear,
And might jump out of the window in despair.

ARNOLPHE

Bring her to me: I'll take her away from here
Posthaste, this very minute.
      (*To Horace:*)
                  Be of good cheer.
Too much good luck could spoil you; and, as they say
In the proverb, every dog must have his day.

HORACE

What man, O Heaven, was ever betrayed like this,
Or hurled into so hopeless an abyss?

ARNOLPHE, *to Oronte*

Pray don't delay the nuptials—which, dear friend,
I shall be most delighted to attend.

ORONTE

I shan't delay.

SCENE NINE

AGNÈS, ALAIN, GEORGETTE, ORONTE, ENRIQUE,
ARNOLPHE, HORACE, CHRYSALDE

ARNOLPHE

Come, come, my pretty child,
You who are so intractable and wild.
Here is your gallant: perhaps he should receive
A little curtsey from you, as you leave.
(*To Horace:*)
Farewell: your sweet hopes seem to have turned to gall;
But love, my boy, can't always conquer all.

AGNÈS

Horace! Will you let him take me away from you?

HORACE

I'm dazed with grief, and don't know what to do.

ARNOLPHE

Come, chatterbox.

AGNÈS

No. Here I shall remain.

148

[*Act Five · Scene Nine*]

ORONTE

Now, what's the mystery? Will you please explain?
All this is very odd; we're baffled by it.

ARNOLPHE

When I've more time, I'll gladly clarify it.
Till then, good-bye.

ORONTE

      Where is it you mean to go?
And why won't you tell us what we ask to know?

ARNOLPHE

I've told you that, despite your stubborn son,
You ought to hold the wedding.

ORONTE

        It shall be done.
But weren't you told that his intended spouse
Is the young woman who's living in your house—
The long-lost child of that dear Angélique
Who secretly was married to Enrique?
What, then, did your behavior mean just now?

CHRYSALDE

His words amazed me, too, I must allow.

[*Act Five · Scene Nine*]

ARNOLPHE

What? What?

CHRYSALDE

My sister married secretly;
Her daughter's birth was kept from the family.

ORONTE

The child was placed with an old country dame,
Who reared her under a fictitious name.

CHRYSALDE

My sister's husband, beset by circumstance,
Was soon obliged to take his leave of France,

ORONTE

And undergo great trials and miseries
In a strange, savage land beyond the seas,

CHRYSALDE

Where, through his labors, he regained abroad
What here he'd lost through men's deceit and fraud.

ORONTE

Returning home, he sought at once to find
The nurse to whom his child had been consigned,

CHRYSALDE

And the good creature told him, as was true,
That she'd transferred her little charge to you,

ORONTE

Because of your benevolent disposition,
And the dire poverty of her condition.

CHRYSALDE

What's more, Enrique, transported with delight,
Has brought the woman here to set things right.

ORONTE

She'll join us in a moment, and then we'll see
A public end to all this mystery.

CHRYSALDE, *to Arnolphe*

I know that you're in a painful state of mind;
Yet what the Fates have done is not unkind.
Since your chief treasure is a hornless head,
The safest course, for you, is not to wed.

ARNOLPHE, *leaving in a speechless passion*

Oof!

ORONTE

Why is he rushing off without a word?

[*Act Five · Scene Nine*]

HORACE

Father, a great coincidence has occurred.
What in your wisdom you projected, chance
Has wondrously accomplished in advance.
The fact is, Sir, that I am bound already,
By the sweet ties of love, to this fair lady;
It's she whom you have come to seek, and she
For whose sake I opposed your plans for me.

ENRIQUE

I recognized her from the very first,
With such deep joy, I thought my heart would burst.
Dear daughter, let me take you in my embrace.
(*He does so.*)

CHRYSALDE

I have the same urge, Brother, but this place
Will hardly do for private joys like these.
Let us go in, resolve all mysteries,
Commend our friend Arnolphe, and for the rest
Thank Heaven, which orders all things for the best.

THE LEARNED
LADIES

COMEDY IN FIVE ACTS, 1672

For Gilbert Parker

INTRODUCTION

The Learned Ladies resembles *Tartuffe* in that it is the drama of a bourgeois household which has lost its harmony and balance through some recent change. In the case of *Tartuffe*, what has changed is that the head of the house, Orgon, who was formerly a sound and solid man, has succumbed to a sort of specious and menopausal religious frenzy. The whole action of the play follows from this aberration of Orgon's, and the whole familial fabric of affections and responsibilities is shaken before the action is over. In *The Learned Ladies* it is once more—though less obviously—the head of the house to whom the disruption of normal relationships may be traced. Chrysale is a soft, comfort-loving person who speaks too often of "my collars" and "my roast of beef." He considers himself peace-loving and gentle, and his daughter Henriette is so kind as to describe his weakness as good nature; but in fact he is an ineffectual man, given to dreaming of his youth, who has always avoided the unpleasantness of exercising his authority as husband and father. The power vacuum thus created has been fully occupied, not long before the play begins, by Chrysale's wilful wife, Philaminte.

It was an unnatural thing, in the view of Molière's audience, for a wife to assume the husband's dominant role, and this is plainly illustrated by the fact that, in early productions of *Les femmes savantes*, the part of Philaminte was played by a male actor. In usurping the headship of the household, Philaminte has become an unsexed woman or the caricature of a man: instead of quiet authority, she has a vain and impatient coerciveness, and her domestic rule amounts to a reign of terror. Her ambition, and a measure of intelligence, lead her to become a bluestocking and, in emulation of certain great ladies, to turn her house into an academy and salon. She enlists in this program her unmarried sister-in-law, Bélise, and her elder daughter, Armande. The spirited and sensible younger daughter, Henriette, declines to be recruited.

In *Les précieuses ridicules* (1659), Molière had made farcical fun of middle-class young women who aspired to salon life, with its refinements of speech and manner, its witticisms, its "spiritual" gallantries, its madrigals and *bouts-rimés*. As the century grew older, salon habitués became concerned with science and philosophy as well, so that Molière's Learned Ladies of 1672 keep a telescope in the attic and make references to Descartes and Epicurus. The atmosphere, *chez* Philaminte, is above all Platonic. Mind and soul are exalted, the body is scorned, and marriage is viewed with contempt. This ambiance is emotionally convenient for Bélise, who adopts the fantasy that all men are secretly and ethereally in love with her, and who also appeases her balked maternal instinct by schooling the servants in elementary grammar and science. For Armande, membership in her mother's "academy" is a less comfortable fate. Following Philaminte's example, she proclaims a pure devotion to spirit and intellect, and a horror of material and bodily things; but in fact she can neither satisfy herself with intellectual activity nor detach herself from the flesh. She would be a touching figure, as many are who suffer from imperfect idealism, were it not for her pretentiousness and for her jealous spite toward those who enjoy what she has renounced.

The abdication of Chrysale, in other words, has precipitated an abnormal situation in which all of the main characters suffer deformity or strain. Bélise is pacified by her chimeras, but at the cost of a complete divorce from the real feelings of others: when Henriette's suitor, Clitandre, turns to her for help in the play's fourth scene, he might as well be addressing a dead woman. Armande, saddled with an aspiration which is too much for her, is condemned to imposture and envy. Philaminte's bullying insistence on creating an intellectual environment arises not from a true thirst for knowledge but from a desire for personal glory, as well as a rancorous wish (which she shares with Armande) to show men that

> *women may be learnèd if they please,*
> *And found, like men, their own academies.*

Because of the ruthless egoism of her project, and its spirit of revenge, Philaminte suppresses in herself the magnanimity which truly belongs to her nature, and which flashes out briefly in the final scene of the play. Her vanity may also be blamed for the blindness with which she admires the egregious pedant Trissotin,

and the heartlessness with which she presses Henriette to marry
him against her wishes.

And what of Henriette? Is she, as one French critic has said,
a "hateful girl" given to false humility, cutting ironies, and banal
conceptions of life? Certainly not. I am of Arthur Tilley's
opinion, that "her simplicity, her directness, and above all, her
sense of humor, make her the most delightful of Molière's young
women." She is far more intelligent and witty than her high-
falutin sister, Armande; she is filial without being spiritless;
independent without being rebellious; admirable in accepting
the fact that she is her lover's second choice; noble in her readi-
ness to release him from what temporarily seems a bad bargain.
To find any of her speeches abrasive is to forget her embattled
and near-desperate position as a younger daughter under pressure
from three variously demented women. We must judge her as
we would a noncollaborative citizen of some occupied country.
Defending herself against Armande, she banters and teases; with
her mother, she sometimes plays dumb or dull; to Clitandre, she
gives blunt and practical strategic advice; in her bold confronta-
tion with Trissotin, she proves a cunning debater, and concludes
with an understandable asperity. In all of this, she shows her
resourcefulness and pluck, but each tactic necessarily entails a
temporary distortion of her nature in reaction to circumstances.
Of Clitandre, too, it may be supposed that the situation exag-
gerates some of his attitudes, and turns him into more of a ranter
than he would usually be.

The Learned Ladies comes as close to being a satiric play as
does anything in Molière's *oeuvre*; yet here as everywhere he
subordinates satire to the comic spirit, which is less interested in
excoriating human error than in affirming the fullness of life. As
always in Molière, there lies in the background of the play a clear
and actual France: it is an absolute monarchy with a Catholic
culture and a powerful Church; it is characterized by strong
class distinctions; in it, all social or familial roles, such as the
father's ruling function in any household, are plain matters of
natural law; it is a highly centralized state, and life at court or in
Paris is very different from life in the provinces. Other basic
aspects of Molière's France might be cited; suffice it, however,
to add that behind this particular play (as behind *The Misan-
thrope*) there also lies the Paris of social and literary cliques and

salons, an élite world which considered itself more elegant than the court. Our understanding of the characters in *The Learned Ladies* is partially shaped by an awareness of the real France beyond them: we note, for instance, that for the upper-middle-class Philaminte the conducting of a salon is a form of social climbing, and that it gratifies her to hear Trissotin recite under her roof a sonnet which has lately pleased "a certain princess." The life of the characters does *not*, however, consist in the satiric indication of real persons belonging to the salon world of Paris; their vitality and depth result, as I have been trying to suggest, from their intense interplay with each other, and from the way in which an unbalanced family situation has warped, divided, or challenged their personalities. We look *at* and *into* Philaminte or Armande, not *through* them.

To this rule there are a couple of apparent exceptions. The name of Philaminte's salon guest Trissotin was, for the seventeenth-century ear, inevitably suggestive of Molière's contemporary Charles Cotin. A member of the French Academy and a frequenter of the most brilliant salons, the Abbé Cotin was a prolific writer of occasional verse, who had more than once satirically attacked Molière and his friend Boileau. Molière avenged himself by naming an unattractive character Trissotin ("thrice-a-fool"), and also by having that character recite as his own work two vulnerably arch poems of Cotin's composition. In Vadius, with whom Trissotin has a literary spat in Act III, audiences easily recognized a reference to the distinguished scholar Gilles Ménage, who made verses in French, Italian, Latin, and Greek, and had once, by several accounts, quarreled with Cotin over the merits of one of the latter's poems. Vadius and Trissotin resemble Ménage and Cotin in the above respects, and one might add that Ménage was well known for the peremptoriness of his aesthetic judgments, and Cotin for being vain of his literary productions. But there the resemblances stop. When *Les femmes savantes* was first acted, Cotin was a sixty-eight-year-old man in holy orders, and could not possibly be confused with the fortune-hunting Trissotin of Act V. No more was Vadius intended as a true portrait of Ménage. Though French audiences of 1672 could enjoy Molière's incidental thrusts as we cannot, the figures of Trissotin and Vadius were finally for them, as for us, two fictional sketches of salon wits. Satire, then, is a secondary and local effect in this play, and the two wits, though less complex than certain other characters, share the same fictional world with them, and serve the same plot and theme.

Plot, in Molière, is best not taken too hard. We should not hold our breaths, toward the close of *Tartuffe*, over the danger that Orgon will lose his property; Molière was not, after all, writing bourgeois melodrama. And neither *The School for Wives* nor *The Learned Ladies* should make us bite our nails for fear that Agnès or Henriette will be forced to marry the wrong man. The use of plot in Molière is, as W. G. Moore has said, "to present an abstract issue in concrete pictures"; the plot is there to shuffle the characters around, providing us with all the confrontations and revelations that are necessary to depict a comic deformity and to define it by contrast to saner behaviors. From this transpires the play's question or theme—which is, in the case of *The Learned Ladies*, the right relation of art and learning to everyday life.

Every major figure in the play, whether male or female, somehow embodies that theme, and the men have their fair share of odiousness and folly. Chrysale, expressing an attitude that many of his original audience would have endorsed, holds that women's "only study and philosophy" should be the rearing of children, the training of servants, the keeping of household accounts, and the making of trousseaus. Nor is he more intellectually ambitious for himself: while there may be nothing scandalous about his indifference to the revolutions of Saturn, he is thoroughly philistine in his scorn of all books save the heavy Plutarch in which he presses his collars. Chrysale's brother, Ariste, is actually more of a catalyst than a character, but one or two of his speeches share Chrysale's distaste for pedantry and for "besotted" intellectuality in women; and the kitchen maid, Martine, vehemently supports her master's aversion to having a bookworm for a son-in-law. None of these persons, of course, speaks for Molière: Ariste's remarks are conditioned by his role as Clitandre's advocate; Chrysale is self-centered and hidebound, and appeals to us only through his wholesome sympathy with young love; Martine has a certain instinctual wisdom, but can scarcely be trusted to appreciate the value that education might have for her betters. And yet we side with this faction, and second what is valid in their speeches, because the "learned ladies" are so ill-motivated and their heroes—Trissotin and Vadius—so appalling. Philaminte, Bélise, and Armande lack, as I have said, any real vocation for the life of the mind, and Act III demonstrates this in numerous ways. By their continual interruption of Trissotin's verses, the ladies show that they have small interest in poetry proper; by their fatuous praise of Trissotin's verses, they show that they have no taste. The "learning" they display is skimpy and ludicrous, and their dreams of an academy have less to do with knowledge than with self-assertion and celebrity. Finally, the scenes with Trissotin and Vadius are so full of coquetry, so charged with repressed sexuality, as to prove the ladies unfitted to be vestals of science and of the spirit. All this being the case, Philaminte and her associates represent a false and fruitless intellectual pretension which entails neglect of all the normal self-realizations and responsibilities of bourgeois women. As for Trissotin's relation to the theme of this play, he is someone for whom learning, or, rather, a literary career, has become the whole of life. Regarding the poems which he dedicates to "Irises and Phyllises," he assures Henriette that

My mind speaks in those verses, not my heart.

But in fact this desiccated man has no heart, and for all his mixing in society, he is perfectly antisocial in the sense of being perfectly selfish; all of his attentions and flatteries to Philaminte's circle, all of his intrigues for dowry or pension, are for the benefit of a self which consists wholly of literary vanity and the pursuit of reputation. Literature and thought, for such a man, are unreal because unrelated to human feeling; in consequence, his life is vicious and his verse is dead.

The healthiest attitudes toward the play's theme are embodied in, and expressed by, Clitandre and Henriette. In respect of two repeated topics, spirituality and language, they represent an agreeable median position. Philaminte and Armande urge a life of pure intellect, and Bélise will have nothing to do with "extended substance"; Chrysale, at the other extreme, identifies himself with his body (*mon corps est moi-même*); but in Act IV, Scene 2, Clitandre firmly tells Armande that he has "both a body and a spirit," and Henriette has already proven the same of herself in the first scene of the play. In regard to language, we have at one extreme the pungent, direct, but limited and ungrammatical speech of Martine; at the other, we have the stifling or prissy rules of the proposed academy, the substanceless flatteries and phrase-making of Trissotin and Vadius, and the absolute dissociation of style and function in Philaminte's proposal that a French marriage contract express the dowry "in talent and drachma," and be dated in "ides and calends." (Since Philaminte twice upbraids the notary for his barbaric style, it is amusing that she is here proposing the use of literal barbarisms.) Though Henriette's speech is at times strategically flat, and though Clitandre, when aroused, can rattle on for thirty lines like Hotspur, their discourse is, on the whole, straightforward, pithy, sprightly, and graceful, and amounts to the best employment of language in the play. The virtues of Clitandre and Henriette are not all to be discovered in some middle ground, however: for instance, despite all the high-minded talk of others, it is they who, in the final scene, represent the extreme of active unselfishness in *Les femmes savantes*.

It is possible to exaggerate the play's anti-intellectualism. One should remember that the action takes place not in the university, the church, a great salon, or the manor house of Madame de Sévigné, but in an upper-bourgeois milieu, where an ill-founded pursuit of the semblance of culture can pervert all of the norms of life. Molière does not deny that there may be truly learned men and women, or true literati like Boileau, and he has Clitandre speak of persons of genuine wit and brain who are not unwelcome at the court. If the pseudo-intellectuality of the "learned ladies" were not so flamboyant, and Clitandre and Henriette so occupied with resisting it, one would more readily notice that the young lovers are literate people who read poetry (Trissotin's, for example) and judge it with some accuracy. Clitandre, it should be observed, is not unfamiliar with the scholarship of Rasius and Baldus, and is capable of criticizing the Platonic separation of body and soul. He and Henriette are in fact witty, intelligent, tasteful, and independent-minded; yet they do not feel that the cultivation of the mind should estrange one from life's basic fulfillments and duties. Neither, clearly, does Molière.

Clitandre's assertion that "A woman should know something . . . / Of every subject" was a quite liberal sentiment for its day, but we will not now recognize it as such unless *The Learned Ladies* is read (or mounted) quite strictly "in period."

[*Introduction*]

Molière is a timeless author in the sense that his art, owing to its clarity and its concern with human fundamentals, is not only readily enjoyed by readers and audiences three centuries after his death, but is often, I think, taken pretty much as it was meant to be taken. This freshness of Molière, his present accessibility, has lately misled some theatrical companies into detaching his art from its temporal background, and giving it the kind of "updating" which involves absurd anachronisms and the loss of meaning through the loss of a credible social frame. Not long ago, I saw a production that aimed to make *Tartuffe* "relevant" by dressing the title character in the sheets and beads of a guru, and having the action take place around a family swimming pool in California. The attempt at topicality was, of course, doomed from the start: it was young people who, in the latter 1960's, were succumbing to the influence of gurus, whereas in Molière's play that is not the situation at all: the children, Damis and Mariane, regard Tartuffe as a fraud, and it is their middle-aged father who is taken in. Not only did the production not mesh with current events, as the director had hoped it would seem to do; it was also miserably confusing, amongst other things, to hear a guru uttering Tartuffe's speeches, which are full of Christian scriptural and liturgical echoes, as well as seventeenth-century Jesuit terminology. More recently, a Boston company based a regrettable "modern-dress" production of *The Misanthrope* on the supposition that Alceste's demand for frankness in social intercourse resembles the demand, lately made by our youth culture, that one "tell it like it is." As a result, the play began with Alceste's entering a twentieth-century American living room in hippie attire, a ten-speed bicycle under his arm. The reader will imagine how implausibly such a figure inhabited the world of the text, where people are addressed as Sir and Madam, where duelling is a serious matter, and where continual reference is made to viscounts, marquesses, and the court of Versailles. I hope that no presenter of this new translation will wish, by means of contemporary costume and set, to attempt a violent conflation of Molière's drama with the current women's movement. And I hope that all readers of this text will envision it in a just historical perspective: Clitandre's liberalism. Henriette's attractively balanced nature, the grotesqueness of the bluestockings, and every nuance of this excellent comedy will then be there to be seen.

Sincere thanks are owed to my colleague Morton Briggs, who urged me to undertake this translation and was so kind as to read it over. I must also thank my wife, and Sonja and William Jay Smith, for their goodness in criticizing both the text and these remarks.

CHARACTERS

CHRYSALE, a well-to-do bourgeois

PHILAMINTE, Chrysale's wife

ARMANDE and ⎱ daughters of Chrysale
HENRIETTE ⎰ and Philaminte

ARISTE, Chrysale's brother

BÉLISE, Chrysale's sister

CLITANDRE, Henriette's suitor

TRISSOTIN, a wit

VADIUS, a scholar

MARTINE, kitchen-maid

LÉPINE, a servant

JULIEN, valet to Vadius

A NOTARY

The scene: Chrysale's house in Paris

ACT 1

SCENE ONE

ARMANDE

What, Sister! Are you truly of a mind
To leave your precious maidenhood behind,
And give yourself in marriage to a man?
Can you be harboring such a vulgar plan?

HENRIETTE

Yes, Sister.

ARMANDE

Yes, you say! When have I heard
So odious and sickening a word?

HENRIETTE

Why does the thought of marriage so repel you?

ARMANDE

Fie, fie! For shame!

HENRIETTE

But what—

ARMANDE

For shame, I tell you!
Can you deny what sordid scenes are brought
To the mind's eye by that distasteful thought,
What coarse, degrading images arise,
What shocking things it makes one visualize?
Do you not shudder, Sister, and grow pale
At what this thought you're thinking would entail?

HENRIETTE

It would entail, as I conceive it, one
Husband, some children, and a house to run;
In all of which, it may as well be said,
I find no cause for loathing or for dread.

ARMANDE

Alas! Such bondage truly appeals to you?

HENRIETTE

At my young age, what better could I do
Than join myself in wedded harmony
To one I love, and who in turn loves me,
And through the deepening bond of man and wife
Enjoy a blameless and contented life?
Does such a union offer no attractions?

ARMANDE

Oh dear, you crave such squalid satisfactions!
How can you choose to play a petty role,
Dull and domestic, and content your soul
With joys no loftier than keeping house
And raising brats, and pampering a spouse?

Let common natures, vulgarly inclined,
Concern themselves with trifles of that kind.
Aspire to nobler objects, seek to attain
To keener joys upon a higher plane,
And, scorning gross material things as naught,
Devote yourself, as we have done, to thought.
We have a mother to whom all pay honor
For erudition; model yourself upon her;
Yes, prove yourself her daughter, as I have done,
Join in the quest for truth that she's begun,
And learn how love of study can impart
A sweet enlargement to the mind and heart.
Why marry, and be the slave of him you wed?
Be married to philosophy instead,
Which lifts us up above mankind, and gives
All power to reason's pure imperatives,
Thus rendering our bestial natures tame
And mastering those lusts which lead to shame.
A love of reason, a passion for the truth,
Should quite suffice one's heart in age or youth,
And I am moved to pity when I note
On what low objects certain women dote.

HENRIETTE

But Heaven, in its wise omnipotence,
Endows us all with differing gifts and bents,
And all souls are not fashioned, I'm afraid,
Of the stuff of which philosophers are made.
If yours was born for soaring to the heights
Of learning, and for speculative flights,
My own weak spirit, Sister, has from birth
Clung to the homelier pleasures of the earth.
Let's not oppose what Heaven has decreed,
But simply follow where our instincts lead.
You, through the towering genius you possess,
Shall dwell in philosophic loftiness,

While my prosaic nature, here below,
Shall taste such joys as marriage can bestow.
Thus, though our lives contrast with one another,
We each shall emulate our worthy mother—
You, in your quest for rational excellence,
I, in the less refined delights of sense;
You, in conceptions lofty and ethereal,
I, in conceptions rather more material.

ARMANDE

Sister, the person whom one emulates
Ought to be followed for her finer traits.
If someone's worthy to be copied, it's
Not for the way in which she coughs and spits.

HENRIETTE

You and your intellect would not be here
If Mother's traits had all been fine, my dear,
And it's most fortunate for you that she
Was not wed solely to philosophy.
Relent, and tolerate in me, I pray,
That urge through which you saw the light of day,
And do not bid me be like you, and scorn
The hopes of some small scholar to be born.

ARMANDE

Your mind, I see, is stupidly contrary,
And won't give up its stubborn wish to marry.
But tell me, do, of this intended match:
Surely it's not Clitandre you aim to catch?

HENRIETTE

Why not? Of what defects could one accuse him?
Would I be vulgar if I were to choose him?

[*Act One · Scene One*]

ARMANDE

No. But I don't think much of your design
To lure away a devotee of mine;
Clitandre, as the world well knows, has sighed
And yearned for me, and sought me as his bride.

HENRIETTE

Yes; but such sighs, arising as they do
From base affections, are as naught to you;
Marriage is something you have risen above,
And fair philosophy has all your love.
Since, then, Clitandre isn't necessary
To your well-being, may he and I not marry?

ARMANDE

Though reason bids us shun the baits of sense,
We still may take delight in compliments;
We may refuse a man, yet be desirous
That still he pay us homage, and admire us.

HENRIETTE

I never sought to make him discontinue
His worship of the noble soul that's in you;
But once you had refused him, I felt free
To take the love which he then offered me.

ARMANDE

When a rejected suitor, full of spite,
Claims to adore you, can you trust him quite?
Do you really think he loves you? Are you persuaded
That his intense desire for me has faded?

173

HENRIETTE

Yes, Sister, I believe it; he's told me so.

ARMANDE

Sister, you're gullible; as you should know,
His talk of leaving me and loving you
Is self-deceptive bluster, and quite untrue.

HENRIETTE

Perhaps; however, Sister, if you'd care
To learn with me the facts of this affair,
I see Clitandre coming; I'm sure, my dear,
That if we ask, he'll make his feelings clear.

SCENE TWO

CLITANDRE, ARMANDE, HENRIETTE

HENRIETTE

My sister has me in uncertainties
As to your heart's affections. If you please,
Clitandre, tell us where your feelings lie,
And which of us may claim you—she or I.

ARMANDE

No, I'll not join in making you reveal
So publicly the passion which you feel;
You are, I'm sure, reluctant to confess
Your private feelings under such duress.

CLITANDRE (*to Armande*)

Madam, my heart, unused to sly pretense,
Does not reluct to state its sentiments;
I'm not at all embarrassed, and can proclaim
Wholeheartedly, without reserve or shame,
That she whom I most honor, hold most dear,
And whose devoted slave I am . . .
                    (*Gesturing toward Henriette*)
                                        is here.
Take no offense; you've nothing to resent:
You've made your choice, and so should be content.
Your charms enthralled me once, as many a sigh

And warm profession served to testify;
I offered you a love which could not fade,
Yet you disdained the conquest you had made.
Beneath your tyrant gaze, my soul has borne
A hundred bitter slights, and every scorn,
Till, wearying at last of whip and chain,
It hungered for a bondage more humane.
Such have I found, *Madame*, in these fair eyes,
　　　(*Gesturing once more toward Henriette*)
Whose kindness I shall ever love and prize:
They have not spurned the man you cast aside,
And, warmed by their regard, my tears have dried.
Now nothing could persuade me to be free
Of this most amiable captivity,
And I entreat you, Madam, do not strive
To cause my former feelings to revive,
Or sway my heart as once you did, for I
Propose to love this lady till I die.

ARMANDE

Well, Sir! What makes you fancy that one might
Regard you with a jealous appetite?
You're fatuous indeed to harbor such
A thought, and very brash to say as much.

HENRIETTE

Steady now, Sister. Where's that discipline
Of soul which reins one's lower nature in,
And keeps one's temper under firm command?

ARMANDE

And you, dear: are your passions well in hand
When you propose to wed a man without
The leave of those who brought your life about?

You owe your parents a complete submission,
And may not love except by their permission;
Your heart is theirs, and you may not bestow it;
To do so would be wicked, and you know it.

HENRIETTE

I'm very grateful to be thus instructed
In how these matters ought to be conducted.
And just to prove to you that I've imbibed
Your teachings, I shall do as you've prescribed:
Clitandre, I should thank you if you went
And gained from my dear parents their consent,
So that, without the risk of wickedness,
I could return the love which you profess.

CLITANDRE

Now that I have your gracious leave, I'll bend
My every effort towards that happy end.

ARMANDE

You look triumphant, Sister, and appear
To think me vexed by what has happened here.

HENRIETTE

By no means, Sister. I well know how you've checked
Your senses with the reins of intellect,
And how no foolish weakness could disturb
A heart so disciplined by wisdom's curb.
I'm far from thinking you upset; indeed,
I know you'll give me the support I need,
Help win my parents to Clitandre's side,
And speed the day when I may be his bride.
Do lend your influence, Sister, to promote—

ARMANDE

What childish teasing, Sister! And how you gloat
At having made a cast-off heart your prize!

HENRIETTE

Cast-off or not, it's one you don't despise.
Had you the chance to get it back from me,
You'd gladly pick it up on bended knee.

ARMANDE

I shall not stoop to answer that. I deem
This whole discussion silly in the extreme.

HENRIETTE

It is indeed, and you do well to end it.
Your self-control is great, and I commend it.

SCENE THREE

CLITANDRE, HENRIETTE

HENRIETTE

Your frank avowal left her quite unnerved.

CLITANDRE

Such frankness was no less than she deserved;
Given her haughty airs and foolish pride,
My blunt words were entirely justified.
But now, since you have given me leave, I'll seek
Your father—

HENRIETTE

        It's to Mother you should speak.
My gentle father would say yes, of course,
But his decrees, alas, have little force;
Heaven blessed him with a mild, concessive soul
Which yields in all things to his wife's control.
It's she who rules the house, requiring him
To treat as law her every royal whim.
I wish that you were more disposed to please
My mother, and indulge my Aunt Bélise,
By humoring their fancies, and thereby
Making them view you with a kindly eye.

CLITANDRE

My heart's too frank for that; I could not praise,
Even in your sister, such outlandish ways,
And female sages aren't my cup of tea.
A woman should know something, I agree,
Of every subject, but this proud desire
To pose as erudite I can't admire.
I like a woman who, though she may know
The answers, does not always let it show;
Who keeps her studies secret and, in fine,
Though she's enlightened, feels no need to shine
By means of pompous word and rare quotation
And brilliance on the slightest provocation.
I much respect your mother; nonetheless,
I can't encourage her in foolishness,
Agree with everything she says, and laud
Her intellectual hero—who's a fraud.
I loathe her Monsieur Trissotin; how can
She so esteem so ludicrous a man,
And class with men of genius and of vision
A dunce whose works meet always with derision,
A bore whose dreadful books end, one and all,
As wrapping paper in some market stall?

HENRIETTE

All that he writes or speaks I find a bore;
I could agree with all you say, and more;
But since the creature has my mother's ear,
He's someone you should cultivate, I fear.
A lover seeks the good opinion of
All who surround the object of his love,
And, so that no one will oppose his passion,
Treats even the house-dog in a courtly fashion.

CLITANDRE

You're right; yet Trissotin, I must admit,
So irks me that there's no controlling it.
I can't, to gain his advocacy, stoop
To praise the works of such a nincompoop.
It was those works which introduced me to him;
Before I ever saw the man, I knew him;
From the vile way he wrote, I saw with ease
What, in the flesh, must be his qualities:
The absolute presumption, the complete
And dauntless nature of his self-conceit,
The calm assurance of superior worth
Which renders him the smuggest man on earth,
So that he stands in awe and hugs himself
Before his volumes ranged upon the shelf,
And would not trade his baseless reputation
For that of any general in the nation.

HENRIETTE

If you could see all that, you've got good eyes.

CLITANDRE

I saw still more; for I could visualize,
By studying his dreadful poetry,
Just what the poet's lineaments must be;
I pictured him so truly that, one day,
Seeing a foppish man in the Palais,
I said, "That's Trissotin, by God!"—and found,
Upon enquiry, that my hunch was sound.

HENRIETTE

What a wild story!

CLITANDRE

Not at all; it's true.
But here's your aunt. If you'll permit me to,
I'll tell her of our hopes, in hopes that she
Will urge your mother to approve of me.

SCENE FOUR

CLITANDRE, BÉLISE

CLITANDRE

Madam, permit a lover's heart to seize
This happy opportunity, if you please,
To tell you of his passion, and reveal—

BÉLISE

Hold, Sir! Don't say too baldly what you feel.
If you belong, Sir, to the ranks of those
Who love me, let your eyes alone disclose
Your sentiments, and do not tell me bluntly
Of coarse desires which only could affront me.
Adore me if you will, but do not show it
In such a way that I'll be forced to know it;
Worship me inwardly, and I shall brook it
If, through your silence, I can overlook it;
But should you dare to speak of it outright,
I'll banish you forever from my sight.

CLITANDRE

My passions, Madam, need cause you no alarms;
It's Henriette who's won me by her charms,
And I entreat your generous soul to aid me
In my design to wed that charming lady.

BÉLISE

Ah, what a subtle dodge; you should be proud;
You're very artful, it must be allowed;
In all the novels that I've read, I've never
Encountered any subterfuge so clever.

CLITANDRE

Madam, I meant no witty indirection;
I've spoken truly of my heart's affection.
By Heaven's will, by ties that cannot part,
I'm bound to Henriette with all my heart;
It's Henriette I cherish, as I've said,
And Henriette whom I aspire to wed.
All that I ask of you is that you lend
Your influence to help me gain that end.

BÉLISE

I well divine the hopes which you have stated,
And how the name you've used should be translated.
A clever substitution, Sir; and I
Shall use the selfsame code in my reply:
"Henriette" disdains to wed, and those who burn
For her must hope for nothing in return.

CLITANDRE

Madam, why make things difficult? Why insist
Upon supposing what does not exist?

BÉLISE

Good heavens, Sir, don't stand on ceremony,
Denying what your looks have often shown me.

184

Let it suffice, Sir, that I am contented
With this oblique approach you have invented,
And that, beneath such decorous disguise,
Your homage is acceptable in my eyes,
Provided that you make no overture
Which is not noble, rarefied, and pure.

CLITANDRE

But—

BÉLISE

    Hush. Farewell. It's time our talk was ended.
I've said, already, more than I intended.

CLITANDRE

You're quite mistaken—

BÉLISE

                    I'm blushing, can't you see?
All this has overtaxed my modesty.

CLITANDRE

I'm hanged if I love you, Madam! This is absurd.

BÉLISE

No, no, I mustn't hear another word.
                    (*She exits.*)

CLITANDRE

The devil take her and her addled brain!
What stubborn fancies she can entertain!
Well, I'll turn elsewhere, and shall hope to find
Support from someone with a balanced mind.

ACT 2

SCENE ONE

ARISTE (*to Clitandre, who is making
his exit*)

Yes, yes, I'll urge and plead as best I can, Sir,
Then hasten back to you and bring his answer.
Lovers! How very much they have to say,
And what extreme impatience they display!
Never—

SCENE TWO

_____

ARISTE

Ah! God be with you, Brother dear.

CHRYSALE

And you, dear Brother.

ARISTE

D'you know what brings me here?

CHRYSALE

No, but I'll gladly learn of it; do tell.

ARISTE

I think you know Clitandre rather well?

CHRYSALE

Indeed; he calls here almost every day.

ARISTE

And what is your opinion of him, pray?

CHRYSALE

He's a man of honor, breeding, wit, and spirit;
I know few lads of comparable merit.

ARISTE

Well, I am here at his request; I'm glad
To learn that you think highly of the lad.

CHRYSALE

I knew his father well, during my stay
In Rome.

ARISTE

Ah, good.

CHRYSALE

A fine man.

ARISTE

So they say.

CHRYSALE

We were both young then, twenty-eight or so,
And a pair of dashing gallants, I'll have you know.

ARISTE

I'm sure of it.

[*Act Two* · *Scene Two*]

CHRYSALE

Oh, those dark-eyed Roman maids!
The whole town talked about our escapades,
And weren't the husbands jealous!

ARISTE

Ho! No doubt!
But let me broach the matter I came about.

SCENE THREE

BÉLISE (*entering quietly and listening*),
CHRYSALE, ARISTE

ARISTE

I'm here to speak for young Clitandre, and let
You know of his deep love for Henriette.

CHRYSALE

He loves my daughter?

ARISTE

            Yes. Upon my honor,
I've never seen such passion; he dotes upon her.

BÉLISE (*to Ariste*)

No, no; I see what's happened. You're unaware
Of the true character of this affair.

ARISTE

What, Sister?

BÉLISE

           Clitandre has misled you, Brother:
The passion which he feels is for another.

ARISTE

Oh, come. He doesn't love Henriette? Then how—

BÉLISE

I'm certain of it.

ARISTE

He said he did, just now.

BÉLISE

Of course.

ARISTE

       He sent me here, please understand,
To ask her father for the lady's hand.

BÉLISE

Splendid.

ARISTE

       What's more, his ardor is so great
That I'm to urge an early wedding date.

BÉLISE

Oh, how delightful; what obliquity!
We use the name of "Henriette," you see,
As a code word and camouflage concealing
The actual object of his tender feeling.
But I'll consent, now, to enlighten you.

194

[*Act Two · Scene Three*]

ARISTE

Well, Sister, since you know so much, please do
Tell us with whom his true affections lie.

BÉLISE

You wish to know?

ARISTE

I do.

BÉLISE

It's I.

ARISTE

You?

BÉLISE

I.

ARISTE

Well, Sister!

BÉLISE

What do you mean by *well?* My word,
Why should you look surprised at what you've heard?
My charms are evident, in my frank opinion,
And more than one heart's under their dominion.
Dorante, Damis, Cléonte, Valère—all these
Are proof of my attractive qualities.

[*Act Two* · *Scene Three*]

ARISTE

These men all love you?

BÉLISE

Yes, with all their might.

ARISTE

They've said so?

BÉLISE

None has been so impolite:
They've worshipped me as one from Heaven above,
And not presumed to breathe a word of love.
Mute signs, however, have managed to impart
The keen devotion of each humble heart.

ARISTE

Damis is almost never seen here. Why?

BÉLISE

His reverence for me has made him shy.

ARISTE

Dorante reviles you in the harshest fashion.

BÉLISE

He's seized, at times, by fits of jealous passion.

ARISTE

Cléonte has lately married; so has Valère.

BÉLISE

That was because I drove them to despair.

ARISTE

Sister, you're prone to fantasies, I fear.

CHRYSALE (*to Bélise*)

Get rid of these chimeras, Sister dear.

BÉLISE

Chimeras! Well! Chimeras, did you say?
I have chimeras! Well, how very gay!
May all your thoughts, dear Brothers, be as clear as
Those which you dared, just now, to call *chimeras!*

SCENE FOUR

CHRYSALE, ARISTE

CHRYSALE

Our sister's mad.

ARISTE

And growing madder daily.
But, once more, let's discuss our business, may we?
Clitandre longs to marry Henriette,
And asks your blessing. What answer shall he get?

CHRYSALE

No need to ask. I readily agree.
His wish does honor to my family.

ARISTE

He has, as you well know, no great amount
Of worldly goods—

CHRYSALE

Ah, gold's of no account:
He's rich in virtue, that most precious ore;
His father and I were bosom friends, what's more.

ARISTE

Let's go make certain that your wife concurs.

CHRYSALE

I've given my consent; no need for hers.

ARISTE

True, Brother; still, 'twould do no harm if your
Decision had her strong support, I'm sure.
Let's both go—

CHRYSALE

    Nonsense, that's a needless move;
I'll answer for my wife. She will approve.

ARISTE

But—

CHRYSALE

 No. Enough. I'll deal with her. Don't worry.
The business will be settled in a hurry.

ARISTE

So be it. I'll go consult with Henriette,
And then—

CHRYSALE

   The thing's as good as done; don't fret.
I'll tell my wife about it, without delay.

SCENE FIVE

MARTINE, CHRYSALE

MARTINE

Ain't that my luck! It's right, what people say—
When you hang a dog, first give him a bad name.
Domestic service! It's a losing game.

CHRYSALE

Well, well, Martine! What's up?

MARTINE

You want to know?

CHRYSALE

Why, yes.

MARTINE

What's up is, Madam's let me go.

CHRYSALE

She's let you go?

MARTINE

Yes, given me the sack.

CHRYSALE

But why? Whatever for?

MARTINE

She says she'll whack
Me black and blue if I don't clear out of here.

CHRYSALE

No, you shall stay; you've served me well, my dear.
My wife's a bit short-tempered at times, and fussy:
But this won't do. I'll—

SCENE SIX

PHILAMINTE, BÉLISE, CHRYSALE, MARTINE

PHILAMINTE (*seeing Martine*)
What! Still here, you hussy!
Be off, you trollop; leave my house this minute,
And mind you never again set foot within it!

CHRYSALE

Gently, now.

PHILAMINTE

No, it's settled.

CHRYSALE

But—

PHILAMINTE

Off with her!

CHRYSALE

What crime has she committed, to incur—

PHILAMINTE

So! You defend the girl!

CHRYSALE

No, that's not so.

PHILAMINTE

Are you taking her side against me?

CHRYSALE

Heavens, no;
I merely asked the nature of her offense.

PHILAMINTE

Would I, without good reason, send her hence?

CHRYSALE

Of course not; but employers should be just—

PHILAMINTE

Enough! I bade her leave, and leave she must.

CHRYSALE

Quite so, quite so. Has anyone denied it?

PHILAMINTE

I won't be contradicted. I can't abide it.

CHRYSALE

Agreed.

[*Act Two · Scene Six*]

PHILAMINTE

If you were a proper husband, you
Would take my side, and share my outrage, too.

CHRYSALE

I do, dear.
(*Turning towards Martine*)
Wench! My wife is right to rid
This house of one who's done the thing you did.

MARTINE

What did I do?

CHRYSALE (*aside*)

Alas, you have me there.

PHILAMINTE

She takes a light view, still, of this affair.

CHRYSALE

What caused your anger? How did all this begin?
Did she break some mirror, or piece of porcelain?

PHILAMINTE

Do you suppose that I'd be angry at her,
And bid her leave, for such a trifling matter?

CHRYSALE (*to Martine*)

What can this mean? (*To Philaminte*) Is the crime, then,
very great?

204

PHILAMINTE

Of course it is. Would I exaggerate?

CHRYSALE

Did she, perhaps, by inadvertence, let
Some vase be stolen, or some china set?

PHILAMINTE

That would be nothing.

CHRYSALE (*to Martine*)

      Blast, girl, what can this be?
      (*To Philaminte*)
Have you caught the chit in some dishonesty?

PHILAMINTE

Far worse than that.

CHRYSALE

Far worse than that?

PHILAMINTE

           Far worse.

CHRYSALE (*to Martine*)

For shame, you strumpet! (*To Philaminte*) Has she been so
  perverse—

[*Act Two* · *Scene Six*]

PHILAMINTE

This creature, who for insolence has no peer,
Has, after thirty lessons, shocked my ear
By uttering a low, plebeian word
Which Vaugelas deems unworthy to be heard.

CHRYSALE

Is *that*—?

PHILAMINTE

And she persists in her defiance
Of that which is the basis of all science—
Grammar! which even the mightiest must obey,
And whose pure laws hold princes in their sway.

CHRYSALE

I was sure she'd done the worst thing under the sun.

PHILAMINTE

What! You don't find it monstrous, what she's done?

CHRYSALE

Oh, yes.

PHILAMINTE

I'd love to hear you plead her case!

CHRYSALE

Not I!

BÉLISE

It's true, her speech is a disgrace.
How long we've taught her language and its laws!
Yet still she butchers every phrase or clause.

MARTINE

I'm sure your preachings is all well and good,
But I wouldn't talk your jargon if I could.

PHILAMINTE

She dares describe as jargon a speech that's based
On reason, and good usage, and good taste!

MARTINE

If people get the point, that's speech to me;
Fine words don't have no use that I can see.

PHILAMINTE

Hark! There's a sample of her style again!
"Don't have no!"

BÉLISE

O ineducable brain!
How futile have our efforts been to teach
Your stubborn mind the rules of proper speech!
You've coupled *don't* with *no*. I can't forgive
That pleonasm, that double negative.

MARTINE

Good Lord, Ma'am, I ain't studious like you;
I just talk plain, the way my people do.

PHILAMINTE

What ghastly solecisms!

BÉLISE

I could faint!

PHILAMINTE

How the ear shudders at the sound of "ain't"!

BÉLISE (*to Martine*)

With ignorance like yours, one struggles vainly.
"Plain" is an adjective; the adverb's "plainly."
Shall grammar be abused by you forever?

MARTINE

Me abuse Gramma? Or Grampa either? Never!

PHILAMINTE

Dear God!

BÉLISE

What I said was "grammar." You misheard.
I've told you about the origin of the word.

MARTINE

Let it come from Passy, Pontoise, or Chaillot;
It's Greek to me.

BÉLISE

Alas, what *do* you know,
You peasant? It is grammar which lays down
The laws which govern adjective and noun,
And verb, and subject.

MARTINE

Madam, I'd just be lying
If I said I knew those people.

PHILAMINTE

Oh, how trying!

BÉLISE

Girl, those are parts of speech, and we must be
At pains to make those parts of speech agree.

MARTINE

Let them agree or squabble, what does it matter?

PHILAMINTE (*to her sister-in-law*)

Ah, mercy, let's be done with all this chatter!
(*To her husband*)
Sir! Will you bid her go and leave me in peace?

CHRYSALE

Yes, yes. (*Aside*) I must give in to her caprice.
(*To Martine*)
Martine, don't vex her further; you'd best depart.

PHILAMINTE

So, you're afraid to wound her little heart!
The hussy! Must you be so sweet and mild?

CHRYSALE

Of course not. (*Loudly*) Wench, be off!
      (*Softly, to Martine*)
               Go, go, poor child.

CHRYSALE

Well, you have had your way, and she is gone;
But I don't think much of the way you've carried on.
The girl is good at what she does, and you've
Dismissed her for a trifle. I don't approve.

PHILAMINTE

Would you have me keep her in my service here
To give incessant anguish to my ear
By constant barbarisms, and the breach
Of every law of reason and good speech,
Patching the mangled discourse which she utters
With coarse expressions from the city's gutters?

BÉLISE

It's true, her talk can drive one out of one's wits.
Each day, she tears dear Vaugelas to bits,
And the least failings of this pet of yours
Are vile cacophonies and non sequiturs.

CHRYSALE

Who cares if she offends some grammar book,
So long as she doesn't offend us as a cook?

If she makes a tasty salad, it seems to me
Her subjects and her verbs need not agree.
Let all her talk be barbarous, if she'll not
Burn up my beef or oversalt the pot.
It's food, not language, that I'm nourished by.
Vaugelas can't teach you how to bake a pie;
Malherbe, Balzac, for all their learnèd rules,
Might, in a kitchen, have been utter fools.

PHILAMINTE

I'm stunned by what you've said, and shocked at seeing
How you, who claim the rank of human being,
Rather than rise on spiritual wings,
Give all your care to base, material things.
This rag, the body—does it matter so?
Should its desires detain us here below?
Should we not soar aloft, and scorn to heed it?

CHRYSALE

My body is myself, and I aim to feed it.
It's a rag, perhaps, but one of which I'm fond.

BÉLISE

Brother, 'twixt flesh and spirit there's a bond;
Yet, as the best minds of the age have stated,
The claims of flesh must be subordinated,
And it must be our chief delight and care
To feast the soul on philosophic fare.

CHRYSALE

I don't know what your soul's been eating of late,
But it's not a balanced diet, at any rate;

You show no womanly solicitude
For—

PHILAMINTE

"Womanly"! That word is old and crude.
It reeks, in fact, of its antiquity.

BÉLISE

It sounds old-fashioned and absurd to me.

CHRYSALE

See here; I can't contain myself; I mean
To drop the mask for once, and vent my spleen.
The whole world thinks you mad, and I am through—

PHILAMINTE

How's that, Sir?

CHRYSALE (*to Bélise*)

Sister, I am addressing *you*.
The least mistake in speech you can't forgive,
But how mistakenly you choose to live!
I'm sick of those eternal books you've got;
In my opinion, you should burn the lot,
Save for that Plutarch where I press my collars,
And leave the studious life to clerks and scholars;
And do throw out, if I may be emphatic,
That great long frightful spyglass in the attic,
And all these other gadgets, and do it soon.
Stop trying to see what's happening in the moon
And look what's happening in your household here,
Where everything is upside down and queer.

For a hundred reasons, it's neither meet nor right
That a woman study and be erudite.
To teach her children manners, overlook
The household, train the servants and the cook,
And keep a thrifty budget—these should be
Her only study and philosophy.
Our fathers had a saying which made good sense:
A woman's polished her intelligence
Enough, they said, if she can pass the test
Of telling a pair of breeches from a vest.
Their wives read nothing, yet their lives were good;
Domestic lore was all they understood,
And all their books were needle and thread, with which
They made their daughters' trousseaus, stitch by stitch.
But women scorn such modest arts of late;
They want to scribble and to cogitate;
No mystery is too deep for them to plumb.
Is there a stranger house in Christendom
Than mine, where women are as mad as hatters,
And everything is known except what matters?
They know how Mars, the moon, and Venus turn,
And Saturn, too, that's none of my concern,
And what with all this vain and far-fetched learning,
They don't know if my roast of beef is burning.
My servants, who now aspire to culture, too,
Do anything but what they're paid to do;
Thinking is all this household thinks about,
And reasoning has driven reason out.
One spoils a sauce, while reading the dictionary;
One mumbles verses when I ask for sherry;
Because they ape the follies they've observed
In you, I keep six servants and am not served.
Just one poor wench remained who hadn't caught
The prevalent disease of lofty thought,
And now, since Vaugelas might find her lacking
In grammar, you've blown up and sent her packing.
Sister (I'm speaking to you, as I said before),

214

These goings-on I censure and deplore.
I'm tired of visits from these pedants versed
In Latin, and that ass Trissotin's the worst.
He's flattered you in many a wretched sonnet;
There's a great swarm of queer bees in his bonnet;
Each time he speaks, one wonders what he's said;
I think, myself, that he's crazy in the head.

PHILAMINTE

Dear God, what brutishness of speech and mind!

BÉLISE

Could particles more grossly be combined,
Or atoms form an aggregate more crass?
And can we be of the same blood? Alas,
I hate myself because we two are kin,
And leave this scene in horror and chagrin.

SCENE EIGHT

PHILAMINTE

Have you other shots to fire, or are you through?

CHRYSALE

I? No, no. No more quarreling. That will do.
Let's talk of something else. As we've heard her state,
Your eldest daughter scorns to take a mate.
She's a philosopher—mind you, I'm not complaining;
She's had the finest of maternal training.
But her younger sister's otherwise inclined,
And I've a notion that it's time to find
A match for Henriette—

PHILAMINTE

                    Exactly, and
I'll now inform you of the match I've planned.
That Trissotin whose visits you begrudge,
And whom you so contemptuously judge,
Is, I've decided, the appropriate man.
If you can't recognize his worth, I can.
Let's not discuss it; it's quite unnecessary;
I've thought things through; it's he whom she should marry.

Don't tell her of my choice, however; I choose
To be the first to let her know the news.
That she will listen to reason I have no doubt,
And if you seek to meddle, I'll soon find out.

SCENE NINE

ARISTE, CHRYSALE

ARISTE

Ah, Brother; your wife's just leaving, and it's clear
That you and she have had a conference here.

CHRYSALE

Yes.

ARISTE

Well, shall Clitandre have his Henriette?
Is your wife willing? Can the date be set?

CHRYSALE

Not altogether.

ARISTE

What, she refuses?

CHRYSALE

No.

ARISTE

Is she wavering, then?

CHRYSALE

I wouldn't describe her so.

ARISTE

What, then?

CHRYSALE

There's someone else whom she prefers.

ARISTE

For a son-in-law?

CHRYSALE

Yes.

ARISTE

Who is this choice of hers?

CHRYSALE

Well . . . Trissotin.

ARISTE

What! That ass, that figure of fun—

CHRYSALE

Who babbles verse and Latin? Yes, that's the one.

ARISTE

Did you agree to him?

CHRYSALE

I? No; God forbid!

ARISTE

What did you say, then?

CHRYSALE

                Nothing; and what I did
Was wise, I think, for it left me uncommitted.

ARISTE

I see! What strategy! How nimble-witted!
Did you, at least, suggest Clitandre, Brother?

CHRYSALE

No. When I found her partial toward another,
It seemed best not to push things then and there.

ARISTE

Your prudence, truly, is beyond compare!
Aren't you ashamed to be so soft and meek?
How can a man be so absurdly weak

As to yield his wife an absolute dominion
And never dare contest her least opinion?

CHRYSALE

Ah, Brother, that's easy enough for you to say.
You've no idea how noisy quarrels weigh
Upon my heart, which loves tranquillity,
And how my wife's bad temper frightens me.
Her nature's philosophic—or that's her claim,
But her tongue's sharp and savage all the same;
All this uplifting thought has not decreased
Her rancorous behavior in the least.
If I cross her even slightly, she will loose
An eight-day howling tempest of abuse.
There's no escape from her consuming ire;
She's like some frightful dragon spitting fire;
And yet, despite her devilish ways, my fear
Obliges me to call her "pet" and "dear."

ARISTE

For shame. That's nonsense. It's your cowardice
Which lets your wife rule over you like this.
What power she has, your weakness has created;
She only rules because you've abdicated;
She couldn't bully you unless you chose,
Like an ass, to let her lead you by the nose.
Come now: despite your timid nature, can
You not resolve for once to be a man,
And, saying "This is how it's going to be,"
Lay down the law, and make your wife agree?
Shall you sacrifice your Henriette to these
Besotted women and their fantasies,
And take for son-in-law, and *heir*, a fool
Who's turned your house into a Latin school,
A pedant whom your dazzled wife extols

As best of wits, most erudite of souls
And peerless fashioner of galiant verse,
And who, in all respects, could not be worse?
Once more I say, for shame: it's ludicrous
To see a husband cringe and cower thus.

CHRYSALE

Yes, you're quite right; I see that I've been wrong.
It's high time, Brother, to be firm and strong,
To take a stand.

ARISTE

Well said.

CHRYSALE

It's base, I know,
To let a woman dominate one so.

ARISTE

Quite right.

CHRYSALE

She's taken advantage of my patience.

ARISTE

She has.

CHRYSALE

And of my peaceful inclinations.

ARISTE

That's true.

CHRYSALE

But, as she'll learn this very day,
My daughter's mine, and I shall have my way
And wed her to a man who pleases me.

ARISTE

Now you're the master, as I'd have you be.

CHRYSALE

Brother, as young Clitandre's spokesman, you
Know where to find him. Send him to me, do.

ARISTE

I'll go this instant.

CHRYSALE

Too long my will's been crossed;
Henceforth I'll be a man, whatever the cost.

ACT 3

SCENE ONE

PHILAMINTE

Let's all sit down and savor, thought by thought,
The verses which our learnèd guest has brought.

ARMANDE

I burn to see them.

BÉLISE

Yes; our souls are panting.

PHILAMINTE (*to Trissotin*)

All that your mind brings forth, I find enchanting.

ARMANDE

For me, your compositions have no peer.

BÉLISE

Their music is a banquet to my ear.

[*Act Three* · *Scene One*]

PHILAMINTE

Don't tantalize your breathless audience.

ARMANDE

Do hurry—

BÉLISE

And relieve this sweet suspense.

PHILAMINTE

Yield to our urging; give us your epigram.

TRISSOTIN (*to Philaminte*)

Madam, 'tis but an infant; still, I am
In hopes that you may condescend to love it,
Since on your doorstep I was delivered of it.

PHILAMINTE

Knowing its father, I can do no other.

TRISSOTIN

Your kind approval, then, shall be its mother.

BÉLISE

What wit he has!

SCENE TWO

HENRIETTE, PHILAMINTE, ARMANDE,
BÉLISE, TRISSOTIN, LÉPINE

PHILAMINTE (*to Henriette, who has
entered and has turned at once to go*)
Ho! Don't rush off like that.

HENRIETTE

I feared I might disrupt your pleasant chat.

PHILAMINTE

Come here, and pay attention, and you shall share
The joy of hearing something rich and rare.

HENRIETTE

I'm no fit judge of elegance in letters;
I leave such heady pastimes to my betters.

PHILAMINTE

That doesn't matter. Stay, and when we're through
I shall reveal a sweet surprise to you.

TRISSOTIN (*to Henriette*)

What need you know of learning and the arts,
Who know so well the way to charm men's hearts?

HENRIETTE

Sir, I know neither; nor is it my ambition—

BÉLISE

Oh, please! Let's hear the infant composition.

PHILAMINTE (*to Lépine*)

Quick, boy, some chairs.
                    (*Lépine falls down in bringing a chair.*)
                                        Dear God, how loutish! Ought you
To fall like that, considering what we've taught you
Regarding equilibrium and its laws?

BÉLISE

Look what you've done, fool. Surely you see the cause?
It was by wrongly shifting what we call
The center of gravity, that you came to fall.

LÉPINE

I saw that when I hit the floor, alas.

PHILAMINTE (*to Lépine, as he leaves*)

Dolt!

TRISSOTIN

It's a blessing he's not made of glass.

ARMANDE

What wit! It never falters!

[*Act Three* · *Scene Two*]

BÉLISE

Not in the least.
(*All sit down.*)

PHILAMINTE

Now then, do serve us your poetic feast.

TRISSOTIN

For such great hunger as confronts me here,
An eight-line dish would not suffice, I fear.
My epigram's too slight. It would be wiser,
I think, to give you first, as appetizer,
A sonnet which a certain princess found
Subtle in sense, delectable in sound.
I've seasoned it with Attic salt throughout,
And you will find it tasty, I have no doubt.

ARMANDE

How could we not?

PHILAMINTE

Let's listen, with concentration.

BÉLISE (*interrupting Trissotin each time
he starts to read*)

My heart is leaping with anticipation.
I'm mad for poetry, and I love it best
When pregnant thoughts are gallantly expressed.

231

[*Act Three* · *Scene Two*]

PHILAMINTE

So long as we talk, our guest can't say a word.

TRISSOTIN

SON—

BÉLISE (*to Henriette*)

Niece, be silent.

ARMANDE

Please! Let the poem be heard.

TRISSOTIN

SONNET TO THE PRINCESS URANIE,
REGARDING HER FEVER

Your prudence, Madam, must have drowsed
When you took in so hot a foe
And let him be so nobly housed,
And feasted and regaled him so.

BÉLISE

A fine first quatrain!

ARMANDE

And the style! How gallant!

PHILAMINTE

For metric flow he has a matchless talent.

ARMANDE

"Your *prudence* must have *drowsed*": a charming touch.

BÉLISE

"So hot a foe" delights me quite as much.

PHILAMINTE

I think that "feasted and regaled" conveys
A sense of richness in so many ways.

BÉLISE

Let's listen to the rest.

TRISSOTIN

Your prudence, Madam, must have drowsed
When you took in so hot a foe
And let him be so nobly housed,
And feasted and regaled him so.

ARMANDE

"Your prudence must have drowsed"!

BÉLISE

"So hot a foe"!

PHILAMINTE

"Feasted and regaled"!

TRISSOTIN

Say what they may, the wretch must go!
From your rich lodging drive away
This ingrate who, as well you know,
Would make your precious life his prey.

BÉLISE

Oh! Pause a moment, I beg you; one is breathless.

ARMANDE

Let us digest those verses, which are deathless.

PHILAMINTE

There's a rare something in those lines which captures
One's inmost heart, and stirs the soul to raptures.

ARMANDE

"Say what they may, the wretch must go!
From your rich lodging drive away . . ."

How apt that is—"rich lodging." I adore
The wit and freshness of that metaphor!

PHILAMINTE

"Say what they may, the wretch must go!"

That "Say what they may" is greatly to my liking.
I've never encountered any words more striking.

ARMANDE

Nor I. That "Say what they may" bewitches me.

234

[Act Three · Scene Two]

BÉLISE

"Say what they may" is brilliant, I agree.

ARMANDE

Oh, to have said it.

BÉLISE

It's a whole poem in a phrase.

PHILAMINTE

But have you fully grasped what it conveys,
As I have?

ARMANDE and BÉLISE

Oh! Oh!

PHILAMINTE

"Say what they may, the wretch must go"!
That means, if people take the fever's side,
Their pleadings should be scornfully denied.

"Say what they may, the wretch must go,
Say what they may, say what they may"!
There's more in that "Say what they may" than first appears.
Perhaps I am alone in this, my dears,
But I see no limit to what that phrase implies.

BÉLISE

It's true, it means a great deal for its size.

PHILAMINTE (*to Trissotin*)

Sir, when you wrote this charming "Say what they may,"
Did you know your own great genius? Can you say
That you were conscious, then, of all the wit
And wealth of meaning we have found in it?

TRISSOTIN

Ah! Well!

ARMANDE

       I'm very fond of "ingrate," too.
It well describes that villain fever, who
Repays his hosts by causing them distress.

PHILAMINTE

In short, the quatrains are a great success.
Do let us have the tercets now, I pray.

ARMANDE

Oh, please, let's once more hear "Say what they may."

TRISSOTIN

Say what they may, the wretch must go!

PHILAMINTE, ARMANDE, and BÉLISE

"Say what they may"!

TRISSOTIN

From your rich lodging drive away . . .

PHILAMINTE, ARMANDE, and BÉLISE

"Rich lodging"!

TRISSOTIN

This ingrate who, as well you know . . .

PHILAMINTE, ARMANDE, and BÉLISE

That "ingrate" of a fever!

TRISSOTIN

Would make your precious life his prey.

PHILAMINTE

"Your precious life"!

ARMANDE and BÉLISE

Ah!

TRISSOTIN

What! Shall he mock your rank, and pay
No deference to the blood of kings?

PHILAMINTE, ARMANDE, and BÉLISE

Ah!

TRISSOTIN

Shall he afflict you night and day,
And shall you tolerate such things?

No! To the baths you must repair,
And with your own hands drown him there.

PHILAMINTE

I'm overcome.

BÉLISE

I'm faint.

ARMANDE

I'm ravished, quite.

PHILAMINTE

One feels a thousand tremors of delight.

ARMANDE

"And shall you tolerate such things?"

BÉLISE

"No! To the baths you must repair . . ."

PHILAMINTE

"And with your own hands drown him there."
Drown him, that is to say, in the bath-water.

ARMANDE

Your verse, at each step, gives some glad surprise.

BÉLISE

Wherever one turns, fresh wonders greet the eyes.

PHILAMINTE

One treads on beauty, wandering through your lines.

ARMANDE

They're little paths all strewn with eglantines.

TRISSOTIN

You find the poem, then—

PHILAMINTE

                  Perfect, and, what's more,
Novel: the like was never done before.

BÉLISE (*to Henriette*)

What, Niece, did not this reading stir your heart?
By saying nothing, you've played a dreary part.

HENRIETTE

We play what parts we're given, here below;
Wishing to be a wit won't make one so.

TRISSOTIN

Perhaps my verses bored her.

[*Act Three* · *Scene Two*]

HENRIETTE

No indeed;
I didn't listen.

PHILAMINTE

The epigram! Please proceed.

TRISSOTIN

CONCERNING A VERMILION COACH, GIVEN
TO A LADY OF HIS ACQUAINTANCE . . .

PHILAMINTE

There's always something striking about his titles.

ARMANDE

They ready us for the wit of his recitals.

TRISSOTIN

Love sells his bonds to me at such a rate . . .

PHILAMINTE, ARMANDE, and BÉLISE

Ah!

TRISSOTIN

I've long since spent the half of my estate;
And when you see this coach, embossed
With heavy gold at such a cost

That all the dazzled countryside
Gapes as my Laïs passes in her pride . . .

PHILAMINTE

Listen to that. "My Laïs." How erudite!

BÉLISE

A stunning reference. So exactly right.

TRISSOTIN

And when you see this coach, embossed
With heavy gold at such a cost
That all the dazzled countryside
Gapes as my Laïs passes in her pride,
Know by that vision of vermilion
That what was mine is now *her* million.

ARMANDE

Oh! Oh! I didn't foresee that final twist.

PHILAMINTE

We have no subtler epigrammatist.

BÉLISE

"Know by that vision of vermilion
That what was mine is now *her* million."

The rhyme is clever, and yet not forced: "*ver*milion, *her*
million."

PHILAMINTE

Since first we met, Sir, I have had the highest
Opinion of you; it may be that I'm biased;
But all you write, to my mind, stands alone.

TRISSOTIN (*to Philaminte*)

If you'd but read us something of your own,
One might reciprocate your admiration.

PHILAMINTE

I've no new poems, but it's my expectation
That soon, in some eight chapters, you may see
The plans I've made for our Academy.
Plato, in his *Republic*, did not go
Beyond an abstract outline, as you know,
But what I've shaped in words, I shall not fail
To realize, in most concrete detail.
I'm much offended by the disrespect
Which men display for women's intellect,
And I intend to avenge us, every one,
For all the slighting things which men have done—
Assigning us to cares which stunt our souls,
And banning our pursuit of studious goals.

ARMANDE

It's too insulting to forbid our sex
To ponder any questions more complex
Than whether some lace is pretty, or some brocade,
And whether a skirt or cloak is nicely made.

BÉLISE

It's time we broke our mental chains, and stated
Our high intent to be emancipated.

TRISSOTIN

My deep respect for women none can deny;
Though I may praise a lady's lustrous eye,
I honor, too, the lustre of her mind.

PHILAMINTE

For that, you have the thanks of womankind;
But there are some proud scholars I could mention
To whom we'll prove, despite their condescension,
That women may be learnèd if they please,
And found, like men, their own academies.
Ours, furthermore, shall be more wisely run
Than theirs: we'll roll all disciplines into one,
Uniting letters, in a rich alliance,
With all the tools and theories of science,
And in our thought refusing to be thrall
To any school, but making use of all.

TRISSOTIN

For method, Aristotle suits me well.

PHILAMINTE

But in abstractions, Plato *does* excel.

ARMANDE

The thought of Epicurus is very keen.

BÉLISE

I rather like his atoms, but as between
A vacuum and a field of subtle matter
I find it easier to accept the latter.

[*Act Three* · *Scene Two*]

TRISSOTIN

On magnetism, Descartes supports my notions.

ARMANDE

I love his falling worlds . . .

PHILAMINTE

And whirling motions!

ARMANDE

I can't wait for our conclaves. We shall proclaim
Discoveries, and they shall bring us fame.

TRISSOTIN

Yes, to your keen minds Nature can but yield,
And let her rarest secrets be revealed.

PHILAMINTE

I can already offer one such rarity:
I have seen men in the moon, with perfect clarity.

BÉLISE

I'm not sure I've seen men, but I can say
That I've seen steeples there, as plain as day.

ARMANDE

To master grammar and physics is our intent,
And history, ethics, verse, and government.

PHILAMINTE

Ethics, which thrills me in so many respects,
Was once the passion of great intellects;
But it's the Stoics to whom I'd give the prize;
They knew that only the virtuous can be wise.

ARMANDE

Regarding language, we aim to renovate
Our tongue through laws which soon we'll promulgate.
Each of us has conceived a hatred, based
On outraged reason or offended taste,
For certain nouns and verbs. We've gathered these
Into a list of shared antipathies,
And shall proceed to doom and banish them.
At each of our learned gatherings, we'll condemn
In mordant terms those words which we propose
To purge from usage, whether in verse or prose.

PHILAMINTE

But our academy's noblest plan of action,
A scheme in which I take deep satisfaction,
A glorious project which will earn the praise
Of all discerning minds of future days,
Is to suppress those *syllables* which, though found
In blameless words, may have a shocking sound,
Which naughty punsters utter with a smirk,
Which, age on age, coarse jesters overwork,
And which, by filthy double meanings, vex
The finer feelings of the female sex.

TRISSOTIN

You have most wondrous plans, beyond a doubt!

245

BÉLISE

You'll see our by-laws, once we've worked them out.

TRISSOTIN

They can't fail to be beautiful and wise.

ARMANDE

By our high standards we shall criticize
Whatever's written, and be severe with it.
We'll show that only we and our friends have wit.
We'll search out faults in everything, while citing
Ourselves alone for pure and flawless writing.

SCENE THREE

LÉPINE, TRISSOTIN, PHILAMINTE, BÉLISE,
ARMANDE, HENRIETTE, VADIUS

LÉPINE (*to Trissotin*)

There's a man outside to see you, Sir; he's wearing
Black, and he has a gentle voice and bearing.

(*All rise.*)

TRISSOTIN

It's that learnèd friend of mine, who's begged me to
Procure for him the honor of meeting you.

PHILAMINTE

Please have him enter; you have our full consent.
     (*Trissotin goes to admit Vadius; Philaminte
        speaks to Armande and Bélise.*)
We must be gracious, and *most* intelligent.
     (*To Henriette, who seeks to leave*)
Whoa, there! I told you plainly, didn't I,
That I wished you to remain with us?

HENRIETTE

              But why?

247

[*Act Three* · *Scene Three*]

PHILAMINTE

Come back, and you shall shortly understand.

TRISSOTIN (*returning with Vadius*)

Behold a man who yearns to kiss your hand.
And in presenting him, I have no fear
That he'll profane this cultured atmosphere:
Among our choicest wits, he quite stands out.

PHILAMINTE

Since you present him, his worth's beyond a doubt.

TRISSOTIN

In classics, he's the greatest of savants,
And knows more Greek than any man in France.

PHILAMINTE (*to Bélise*)

Greek! Sister, our guest knows Greek! How marvelous!

BÉLISE (*to Armande*)

Greek, Niece! Do you hear?

ARMANDE

Yes, Greek! What joy for *us!*

PHILAMINTE

Think of it! Greek! Oh, Sir, for the love of Greek,
Permit us each to kiss you on the cheek.
　　(*Vadius kisses them all save Henriette, who refuses.*)

HENRIETTE

I don't know Greek, Sir; permit me to decline.

PHILAMINTE

I think Greek books are utterly divine.

VADIUS

In my eagerness to meet you, I fear I've come
Intruding on some grave symposium.
Forgive me, Madam, if I've caused confusion.

PHILAMINTE

Ah, Sir, to bring us Greek is no intrusion.

TRISSOTIN

My friend does wonders, too, in verse and prose,
And might well show us something, if he chose.

VADIUS

The fault of authors is their inclination
To dwell upon their works in conversation,
And whether in parks, or parlors, or at table,
To spout their poems as often as they're able.
How sad to see a writer play the extorter,
Demanding oh's and ah's from every quarter,
And forcing any gathering whatever
To tell him that his labored verse is clever.
I've never embraced the folly of which I speak,
And hold the doctrine of a certain Greek
That men of sense, however well endowed,

249

Should shun the urge to read their works aloud.
Still, here are some lines, concerning youthful love,
Which I'd be pleased to hear your judgments of.

TRISSOTIN

For verve and beauty, your verses stand alone.

VADIUS

Venus and all the Graces grace your own.

TRISSOTIN

Your choice of words is splendid, and your phrasing.

VADIUS

Your *ethos* and your *pathos* are amazing.

TRISSOTIN

The polished eclogues which you've given us
Surpass both Virgil and Theocritus.

VADIUS

Your odes are noble, gallant, and refined,
And leave your master Horace far behind.

TRISSOTIN

Ah, but your little love songs: what could be sweeter?

VADIUS

As for your well-turned sonnets, none are neater.

TRISSOTIN

Your deft *rondeaux;* are any poems more charming?

VADIUS

Your madrigals—are any more disarming?

TRISSOTIN

Above all, you're a wizard at *ballades.*

VADIUS

At *bouts-rimés,* you always have the odds.

TRISSOTIN

If France would only recognize your merits—

VADIUS

If the age did justice to its finer spirits—

TRISSOTIN

You'd have a gilded coach in which to ride.

VADIUS

Statues of you would rise on every side.
                    (*To Trissotin*)
Hem! Now for my *ballade.* Please comment on it
In the frankest—

[*Act Three · Scene Three*]

TRISSOTIN

        Have you seen a certain sonnet
About the fever of Princess Uranie?

VADIUS

Yes. It was read to me yesterday, at tea.

TRISSOTIN

Do you know who wrote it?

VADIUS

        No, but of this I'm sure:
The sonnet, frankly, is very, very poor.

TRISSOTIN

Oh? Many people have praised it, nonetheless.

VADIUS

That doesn't prevent its being a sorry mess,
And if you've read it, I know you share my view.

TRISSOTIN

Why no, I don't in the least agree with you;
Not many sonnets boast so fine a style.

VADIUS

God grant I never write a thing so vile!

TRISSOTIN

It couldn't be better written, I contend;
And I should know, because I wrote it, friend.

VADIUS

You?

TRISSOTIN

I.

VADIUS

Well, how this happened I can't explain.

TRISSOTIN

What happened was that you found my poem inane.

VADIUS

When I heard the sonnet, I must have been distrait;
Or perhaps 'twas read in an unconvincing way.
But let's forget it; this *ballade* of mine—

TRISSOTIN

Ballades, I think, are rather asinine.
The form's old-hat; it has a musty smell.

VADIUS

Still, many people like it very well.

TRISSOTIN

That doesn't prevent my finding it dull and flat.

VADIUS

No, but the form is none the worse for that.

TRISSOTIN

The *ballade* is dear to pedants; they adore it.

VADIUS

How curious, then, that you should not be for it.

TRISSOTIN

You see in others your own drab qualities.

(*All rise.*)

VADIUS

Don't see your own in me, Sir, if you please.

TRISSOTIN

Be off, you jingling dunce! Let's end this session.

VADIUS

You scribbler! You disgrace to the profession!

TRISSOTIN

You poetaster! You shameless plagiarist!

[*Act Three* · *Scene Three*]

VADIUS

You ink-stained thief!

PHILAMINTE

Oh, gentlemen! Please desist!

TRISSOTIN (*to Vadius*)

Go to the Greeks and Romans, and pay back
The thousand things you've filched from them, you hack.

VADIUS

Go to Parnassus and confess your guilt
For turning Horace into a crazy-quilt.

TRISSOTIN

Think of your book, which caused so little stir.

VADIUS

And you, Sir, think of your bankrupt publisher.

TRISSOTIN

My fame's established; in vain you mock me so.

VADIUS

Do tell. Go look at the *Satires* of Boileau.

TRISSOTIN

Go look at them yourself.

VADIUS

As between us two,
I'm treated there more honorably than you.
He gives me a passing thrust, and links my name
With several authors of no little fame;
But nowhere do his verses leave you in peace;
His witty attacks upon you never cease.

TRISSOTIN

It's therefore I whom he respects the more.
To him, you're one of the crowd, a minor bore;
You're given a single sword-thrust, and are reckoned
Too insignificant to deserve a second.
But me he singles out as a noble foe
Against whom he must strive with blow on blow,
Betraying, by those many strokes, that he
Is never certain of the victory.

VADIUS

My pen will teach you that I'm no poetaster.

TRISSOTIN

And mine will show you, fool, that I'm your master.

VADIUS

I challenge you in verse, prose, Latin, and Greek.

TRISSOTIN

We'll meet at Barbin's bookshop, in a week.

SCENE FOUR

TRISSOTIN, PHILAMINTE, ARMANDE,
BÉLISE, HENRIETTE

TRISSOTIN (*to Philaminte*)

Forgive me if my wrath grew uncontrolled;
I felt an obligation to uphold
Your judgment of that sonnet he maligned.

PHILAMINTE

I'll try to mend your quarrel; never mind.
Let's change the subject. Henriette, come here.
I've long been troubled because you don't appear
At all endowed with wit or intellect;
But I've a remedy, now, for that defect.

HENRIETTE

Don't trouble, Mother; I wish no remedy.
Learnèd discourse is not my cup of tea.
I like to take life easy, and I balk
At trying to be a fount of clever talk.
I've no ambition to be a parlor wit,
And if I'm stupid, I don't mind a bit.
I'd rather speak in a plain and common way
Than rack my brains for brilliant things to say.

PHILAMINTE

I know your shameful tastes, which I decline
To countenance in any child of mine.
Beauty of face is but a transient flower,
A brief adornment, the glory of an hour,
And goes no deeper than the outer skin;
But beauty of mind endures, and lies within.
I've long sought means to cultivate in you
A beauty such as time could not undo,
And plant within your breast a noble yearning
For higher knowledge and the fruits of learning;
And now, at last, I've settled on a plan,
Which is to mate you with a learnèd man—
                    (*Gesturing toward Trissotin*)
This gentleman, in short, whom I decree
That you acknowledge as your spouse-to-be.

HENRIETTE

I, Mother?

PHILAMINTE

Yes, you. Stop playing innocent.

BÉLISE (*to Trissotin*)

I understand. Your eyes ask my consent
Before you pledge to her a heart that's mine.
Do so. All claims I willingly resign:
This match will bring you wealth and happiness.

TRISSOTIN (*to Henriette*)

My rapture, Madam, is more than I can express:
The honor which this marriage will confer
Upon me—

258

HENRIETTE

Hold! It's not yet settled, Sir;
Don't rush things.

PHILAMINTE

What a reply! How overweening!
Girl, if you dare . . . Enough, you take my meaning.
(*To Trissotin*)
Just let her be. Her mind will soon be changed.

SCENE FIVE

HENRIETTE, ARMANDE

ARMANDE

What a brilliant match our mother has arranged!
She's found for you a spouse both great and wise.

HENRIETTE

Why don't you take him, if he's such a prize?

ARMANDE

It's you, not I, who are to be his bride.

HENRIETTE

For my elder sister, I'll gladly step aside.

ARMANDE

If I, like you, yearned for the wedded state,
I'd take your offer of so fine a mate.

HENRIETTE

If I, like you, were charmed by pedantry,
I'd think the man a perfect choice for me.

[*Act Three* · *Scene Five*]

ARMANDE

Our tastes may differ, Sister, but we still
Owe strict obedience to our parents' will;
Whether or not you're fractious and contrary,
You'll wed the man our mother bids you marry. . . .

SCENE SIX

CHRYSALE, ARISTE, CLITANDRE,
HENRIETTE, ARMANDE

CHRYSALE (*to Henriette, presenting Clitandre*)

Now, Daughter, you shall do as I command.
Take off that glove, and give this man your hand,
And think of him henceforward as the one
I've chosen as your husband and my son.

ARMANDE

In this case, Sister, you're easy to persuade.

HENRIETTE

Sister, our parents' will must be obeyed;
I'll wed the man my father bids me marry.

ARMANDE

Your mother's blessing, too, is necessary.

CHRYSALE

Just what do you mean?

[*Act Three* · *Scene Six*]

ARMANDE

     I much regret to state
That Mother has a rival candidate
For the hand of Henri—

CHRYSALE

     Hush, you chatterer!
Go prate about philosophy with her,
And cease to meddle in what is my affair.
Tell her it's settled, and bid her to beware
Of angering me by making any fuss.
Go on, now.

ARISTE

Bràvo! This is miraculous.

CLITANDRE

How fortunate I am! What bliss! What joy!

CHRYSALE (*to Clitandre*)

Come, take her hand, now. After you, my boy;
Conduct her to her room. (*To Ariste*) Ah, Brother, this is
A tonic to me; think of those hugs, those kisses!
It warms my old heart, and reminds me of
My youthful days of gallantry and love.

ACT 4

SCENE ONE

ARMANDE

Oh, no, she didn't waver or delay,
But, with a flourish, hastened to obey.
Almost before he spoke, she had agreed
To do his bidding, and she appeared, indeed,
Moved by defiance toward her mother, rather
Than deference to the wishes of her father.

PHILAMINTE

I soon shall show her to whose government
The laws of reason oblige her to consent,
And whether it's matter or form, body or soul,
Father or mother, who is in control.

ARMANDE

The least they could have done was to consult you;
It's graceless of that young man to insult you
By trying to wed your child without your blessing.

PHILAMINTE

He's not yet won. His looks are prepossessing,
And I approved his paying court to you;

But I never liked his manners. He well knew
That writing poetry is a gift of mine,
And yet he never asked to hear a line.

SCENE TWO

CLITANDRE (*entering quietly and listening
unseen*), ARMANDE, PHILAMINTE

ARMANDE

Mother, if I were you, I shouldn't let
That gentleman espouse our Henriette.
Not that I care, of course; I do not speak
As someone moved by prejudice or pique,
Or by a heart which, having been forsaken,
Asks vengeance for the wounds which it has taken.
For what I've suffered, philosophy can give
Full consolation, helping one to live
On a high plane, and treat such things with scorn;
But what he's done to you cannot be borne.
Honor requires that you oppose his suit;
Besides, you'd never come to like the brute.
In all our talks, I cannot recollect
His speaking of you with the least respect.

PHILAMINTE

Young whelp!

ARMANDE

   Despite your work's great reputation,
He icily withheld his approbation.

PHILAMINTE

The churl!

ARMANDE

A score of times, I read to him
Your latest poems. He tore them limb from limb.

PHILAMINTE

The beast!

ARMANDE

We quarreled often about your writing.
And you would not believe how harsh, how biting—

CLITANDRE (*to Armande*)

Ah, Madam, a little charity, I pray,
Or a little truthful speaking, anyway.
How have I wronged you? What was the offense
Which makes you seek, by slanderous eloquence,
To rouse against me the distaste and ire
Of those whose good opinion I require?
Speak, Madam, and justify your vicious grudge.
I'll gladly let your mother be our judge.

ARMANDE

Had I the grudge of which I stand accused,
I could defend it, for I've been ill-used.
First love, Sir, is a pure and holy flame
Which makes upon us an eternal claim;

'Twere better to renounce this world, and die,
Than be untrue to such a sacred tie.
Fickleness is a monstrous crime, and in
The moral scale there is no heavier sin.

CLITANDRE

Do you call it fickleness, *Madame*, to do
What your heart's cold disdain has driven me to?
If, by submitting to its cruel laws,
I've wounded you, your own proud heart's the cause.
My love for you was fervent and entire;
For two whole years it burned with constant fire;
My duty, care, and worship did not falter;
I laid my heart's devotion on your altar.
But all my love and service were in vain;
You dashed the hopes I dared to entertain.
If, thus rejected, I made overtures
To someone else, was that my fault, or yours?
Was I inconstant, or was I forced to be?
Did I forsake you, or did you banish me?

ARMANDE

Sir, can you say that I've refused your love
When all I've sought has been to purge it of
Vulgarity, and teach you that refined
And perfect passion which is of the mind?
Can you not learn an ardor which dispenses
Entirely with the commerce of the senses,
Or see how sweetly spirits may be blended
When bodily desires have been transcended?
Alas, your love is carnal, and cannot rise
Above the plane of gross material ties;
The flame of your devotion can't be fed
Except by marriage, and the marriage bed.

How strange is such a love! And oh, how far
Above such earthliness true lovers are!
In their delights, the body plays no part,
And their clear flames but marry heart to heart,
Rejecting all the rest as low and bestial.
Their fire is pure, unsullied, and celestial.
The sighs they breathe are blameless, and express
No filthy hankerings, no fleshliness.
There's no ulterior goal they hunger for.
They love for love's sake, and for nothing more,
And since the spirit is their only care,
Bodies are things of which they're unaware.

CLITANDRE

Well, *I'm* aware, though you may blush to hear it,
That I have both a body and a spirit;
Nor can I part them to my satisfaction;
I fear I lack the power of abstraction
Whereby such philosophic feats are done,
And so my body and soul must live as one.
There's nothing finer, as you say, than these
Entirely spiritual ecstasies,
These marriages of souls, these sentiments
So purified of any taint of sense;
But such love is, for my taste, too ethereal;
I am, as you've complained, a bit material;
I love with all my being, and I confess
That a whole woman is what I would possess.
Need I be damned for feelings of the kind?
With all respect for your high views, I find
That men in general feel my sort of passion,
That marriage still is pretty much in fashion,
And that it's deemed an honorable estate;
So that my asking you to be my mate,
And share with me that good and sweet condition,
Was scarcely an indecent proposition.

ARMANDE

Ah well, Sir: since you thrust my views aside,
Since your brute instincts must be satisfied,
And since your feelings, to be faithful, must
Be bound by ties of flesh and chains of lust,
I'll force myself, if Mother will consent,
To grant the thing on which you're so intent.

CLITANDRE

It's too late, Madam: another's occupied
Your place; if I now took you as my bride,
I'd wrong a heart which sheltered and consoled me
When, in your pride, you'd treated me so coldly.

PHILAMINTE

Sir, do you dream of my consenting to
This other marriage which you have in view?
Does it not penetrate your mind as yet
That I have other plans for Henriette?

CLITANDRE

Ah, Madam, reconsider, if you please,
And don't expose me thus to mockeries;
Don't put me in the ludicrous position
Of having Trissotin for competition.
What a shabby rival! You couldn't have selected
A wit less honored, a pedant less respected.
We've many pseudo-wits and polished frauds
Whose cleverness the time's bad taste applauds,
But Trissotin fools no one, and indeed
His writings are abhorred by all who read.
Save in this house, his work is never praised,
And I have been repeatedly amazed

To hear you laud some piece of foolishness
Which, had you written it, you would suppress.

PHILAMINTE

That's how you judge him. We feel otherwise
Because we look at him with different eyes.

SCENE THREE

TRISSOTIN (*to Philaminte*)

I bring you, Madam, some startling news I've heard.
Last night, a near-catastrophe occurred:
While we were all asleep, a comet crossed
Our vortex, and the Earth was all but lost;
Had it collided with our world, alas,
We'd have been shattered into bits, like glass.

PHILAMINTE

Let's leave that subject for another time;
This gentleman, I fear, would see no rhyme
Or reason in it; it's ignorance he prizes;
Learning and wit are things which he despises.

CLITANDRE

Kindly permit me, Madam, to restate
Your summary of my views: I only hate
Such wit and learning as twist men's brains awry.
Those things are excellent in themselves, but I
Had rather be an ignorant man, by far,
Than learnèd in the way some people are.

TRISSOTIN

Well, as for me, I hold that learning never
Could twist a man in any way whatever.

CLITANDRE

And I assert that learning often breeds
Men who are foolish both in words and deeds.

TRISSOTIN

What a striking paradox!

CLITANDRE

          Though I'm no **wit**,
I'd have no trouble, I think, in proving it.
If arguments should fail, I'm sure I'd find
That living proofs came readily to mind.

TRISSOTIN

The living proofs you gave might not persuade.

CLITANDRE

I'd not look far before my point was made.

TRISSOTIN

I cannot think, myself, of such a case.

CLITANDRE

I can; indeed, it stares me in the face.

TRISSOTIN

I thought it was by ignorance, and not
By learning, Sir, that great fools were begot.

CLITANDRE

Well, you thought wrongly. It's a well-known rule
That no fool's greater than a learnèd fool.

TRISSOTIN

Our common usage contradicts that claim,
Since "fool" and "ignoramus" mean the same.

CLITANDRE

You think those words synonymous? Oh no, Sir!
You'll find that "fool" and "pedant" are much closer.

TRISSOTIN

"Fool" denotes plain and simple foolishness.

CLITANDRE

"Pedant" denotes the same, in fancy dress.

TRISSOTIN

The quest for knowledge is noble and august.

CLITANDRE

But knowledge, in a pedant, turns to dust.

TRISSOTIN

It's clear that ignorance has great charms for you,
Or else you wouldn't defend it as you do.

CLITANDRE

I came to see the charms of ignorance when
I made the acquaintance of certain learnèd men.

TRISSOTIN

Those certain learnèd men, it may turn out,
Are better than certain folk who strut about.

CLITANDRE

The learnèd men would say so, certainly;
But then, those certain folk might not agree.

PHILAMINTE (*to Clitandre*)

I think, Sir—

CLITANDRE

        Madam, spare me, please. This rough
Assailant is already fierce enough.
Don't join him, pray, in giving me a beating.
I shall preserve myself, now, by retreating.

ARMANDE

You, with your brutal taunts, were the offender;
'Twas you—

[*Act Four* · *Scene Three*]

CLITANDRE

More reinforcements! I surrender.

PHILAMINTE

Sir, witty repartee is quite all right,
But personal attacks are impolite.

CLITANDRE

Good Lord, he's quite unhurt, as one can tell.
No one in France takes ridicule so well.
For years he's heard men gibe at him, and scoff,
And in his smugness merely laughed it off.

TRISSOTIN

I'm not surprised to hear this gentleman say
The things he's said in this unpleasant fray.
He's much at court, and as one might expect,
He shares the court's mistrust of intellect,
And, as a courtier, defends with zest
The ignorance that's in its interest.

CLITANDRE

You're very hard indeed on the poor court,
Which hears each day how people of your sort,
Who deal in intellectual wares, decry it,
Complain that their careers are blighted by it,
Deplore its wretched taste, and blame their own
Unhappy failures on that cause alone.
Permit me, Mister Trissotin, with due
Respect for your great name, to say that you
And all your kind would do well to discuss

The court in tones less harsh and querulous;
That the court is not so short of wit and brain
As you and all your scribbling friends maintain;
That all things, there, are viewed with common sense,
That good taste, too, is much in evidence,
And that its knowledge of the world surpasses
The fusty learning of pedantic asses.

TRISSOTIN

It has good taste, you say? If only it had!

CLITANDRE

What makes you say, Sir, that its taste is bad?

TRISSOTIN

What makes me say so? Rasiùs and Baldùs
Do France great honor by what their pens produce,
Yet the court pays these scholars no attention,
And neither of them has received a pension.

CLITANDRE

I now perceive your grievance, and I see
That you've left your own name out, from modesty.
Well, let's not drag it into our debate.
Just tell me: how have your heroes served the State?
What are their writings worth, that they expect
Rewards, and charge the nation with neglect?
Why should they whine, these learnèd friends of yours,
At not receiving gifts and sinecures?
A precious lot they've done for France, indeed!
Their tomes are just what court and country need!
The vanity of such beggars makes me laugh:

Because they're set in type and bound in calf,
They think that they're illustrious citizens;
That the fate of nations hangs upon their pens;
That the least mention of their work should bring
The pensions flocking in on eager wing;
That the whole universe, with one wide stare,
Admires them; that their fame is everywhere,
And that they're wondrous wise because they know
What others said before them, long ago—
Because they've given thirty years of toil
And eyestrain to acquire, by midnight oil,
Some jumbled Latin and some garbled Greek,
And overload their brains with the antique
Obscurities which lie about in books.
These bookworms, with their smug, myopic looks,
Are full of pompous talk and windy unction;
They have no common sense, no useful function,
And could, in short, persuade the human race
To think all wit and learning a disgrace.

PHILAMINTE

You speak most heatedly, and it is clear
What feelings prompt you to be so severe;
Your rival's presence, which seems to irk you greatly—

SCENE FOUR

JULIEN, TRISSOTIN, PHILAMINTE,
CLITANDRE, ARMANDE

JULIEN

The learnèd man who visited you lately,
And whose valet I have the honor to be,
Sends you this note, *Madame*, by way of me.

PHILAMINTE

Whatever the import of this note you bring,
Do learn, my friend, that it's a graceless thing
To interrupt a conversation so,
And that a rightly trained valet would go
To the servants first, and ask them for admission.

JULIEN

Madam, I'll bear in mind your admonition.

PHILAMINTE (*reading*)

"Trissotin boasts, Madam, that he is going to marry your
daughter. Let me warn you that that great thinker is thinking
only of your wealth, and that you would do well to put off
the marriage until you have seen the poem which I am now
composing against him. It is to be a portrait in verse, and I
propose to depict him for you in his true colors. Meanwhile,

I am sending herewith the works of Horace, Virgil, Terence,
and Catullus, in the margins of which I have marked, for
your benefit, all the passages which he has plundered."

Well, well! To thwart the match which I desire,
A troop of enemies has opened fire
Upon this worthy man; but I'll requite
By one swift action their dishonest spite,
And show them all that their combined assault
Has only hastened what they strove to halt.
                    (*To Julien*)
Take back those volumes to your master, and
Inform him, so that he'll clearly understand
Precisely how much value I have set
Upon his sage advice, that Henriette
                (*Pointing to Trissotin*)
Shall wed this gentleman, this very night.
                    (*To Clitandre*)
Sir, you're a friend of the family. I invite
You most sincerely to remain and see
The contract signed, as shortly it shall be.
Armande, you'll send for the notary, and prepare
Your sister for her part in this affair.

ARMANDE

No need for me to let my sister know;
This gentleman, I'm sure, will quickly go
To tell her all the news, and seek as well
To prompt her saucy spirit to rebel.

PHILAMINTE

We'll see by whom her spirit will be swayed;
It doesn't suit me to be disobeyed.

SCENE FIVE

ARMANDE, CLITANDRE

ARMANDE

I'm very sorry for you, Sir; it seems
Things haven't gone according to your schemes.

CLITANDRE

Madam, I mean to do my very best
To lift that weight of sorrow from your breast.

ARMANDE

I fear, Sir, that your hopes are not well-grounded.

CLITANDRE

It may be that your fear will prove ill-founded.

ARMANDE

I hope so.

CLITANDRE

I believe you; nor do I doubt
That you'll do all you can to help me out.

284

ARMANDE

To serve your cause shall be my sole endeavor.

CLITANDRE

For that, you'll have my gratitude forever.

SCENE SIX

CHRYSALE, ARISTE, HENRIETTE, CLITANDRE

CLITANDRE

I shall be lost unless you help me, Sir:
Your wife's rejected my appeals to her,
And chosen Trissotin for her son-in-law.

CHRYSALE

Damn it, what ails the woman? I never saw
What in this Trissotin could so attract her.

ARISTE

He versifies in Latin, and that's a factor
Which makes him, in her view, the better man.

CLITANDRE

To marry them tonight, Sir, is her plan.

CHRYSALE

Tonight?

CLITANDRE

Tonight.

CHRYSALE

Her plan, then, will miscarry.
I promise that, tonight, you two shall marry.

CLITANDRE

She's having a contract drawn by the notary.

CHRYSALE

Well, he shall draw another one for me.

CLITANDRE (*indicating Henriette*)

Armande has orders to inform this lady
Of the wedding match for which she's to be ready.

CHRYSALE

And I inform her that, by my command,
It's you on whom she shall bestow her hand.
This is my house, and I shall make it clear
That I'm the one and only master here.
                    (*To Henriette*)
Wait, Daughter; we'll join you when our errand's done.
Come, Brother, follow me; you too, my son.

HENRIETTE (*to Ariste*)

Please keep him in this mood, whatever you do.

ARISTE

I'll do my utmost for your love and you.

SCENE SEVEN

HENRIETTE, CLITANDRE

CLITANDRE

Whatever aid our kind allies may lend,
It's your true heart on which my hopes depend.

HENRIETTE

As to my heart, of that you may be sure.

CLITANDRE

If so, my own is happy and secure.

HENRIETTE

I must be strong, so as not to be coerced.

CLITANDRE

Cling to our love, and let them do their worst.

HENRIETTE

I'll do my best to make our cause prevail;
But if my hope of being yours should fail,
And if it seems I'm to be forced to marry,
A convent cell shall be my sanctuary.

CLITANDRE

Heaven grant that you need never give to me
Such painful proof of your fidelity.

ACT 5

SCENE ONE

HENRIETTE

It seems to me that we two should confer
About this contemplated marriage, Sir,
Since it's reduced our household to dissension.
Do give my arguments your kind attention.
I know that you expect to realize,
By wedding me, a dowry of some size;
Yet money, which so many men pursue,
Should bore a true philosopher like you,
And your contempt for riches should be shown
In your behavior, not in words alone.

TRISSOTIN

It's not in wealth that your attraction lies:
Your sparkling charms, your soft yet flashing eyes,
Your airs, your graces—it is these in which
My ravished heart perceives you to be rich,
These treasures only which I would possess.

HENRIETTE

I'm honored by the love which you profess,
Although I can't see what I've done to earn it,
And much regret, Sir, that I can't return it.
I have the highest estimation of you,

But there's one reason why I cannot love you.
A heart's devotion cannot be divided,
And it's Clitandre on whom my heart's decided.
I know he lacks your merits, which are great,
That I'm obtuse to choose him for my mate,
That you should please me by your gifts and wit;
I know I'm wrong, but there's no help for it;
Though reason chides me for my want of sense,
My heart clings blindly to its preference.

TRISSOTIN

When I am given your hand and marriage vow,
I'll claim the heart Clitandre possesses now,
And I dare hope that I can then incline
That heart, by sweet persuasions, to be mine.

HENRIETTE

No, no: first love, Sir, is too strong a feeling.
All your persuasions could not prove appealing.
Let me, upon this point, be blunt and plain,
Since nothing I shall say could cause you pain.
The fires of love, which set our hearts aglow,
Aren't kindled by men's merits, as you know.
They're most capricious; when someone takes our eye,
We're often quite unable to say why.
If, Sir, our loves were based on wise selection,
You would have all my heart, all my affection;
But love quite clearly doesn't work that way.
Indulge me in my blindness, then, I pray,
And do not show me, Sir, so little mercy
As to desire that others should coerce me.
What man of honor would care to profit by
A parent's power to make a child comply?
To win a lady's hand by such compulsion,
And not by love, would fill him with revulsion.

Don't, then, I beg you, urge my mother to make
Me bow to her authority for your sake.
Take back the love you offer, and reserve it
For some fine woman who will more deserve it.

TRISSOTIN

Alas, what you command I cannot do.
I'm powerless to retract my love for you.
How shall I cease to worship you, unless
You cease to dazzle me with loveliness,
To stun my heart with beauty, to enthrall—

HENRIETTE

Oh, come, Sir; no more nonsense. You have all
These Irises and Phyllises whose great
Attractiveness your verses celebrate,
And whom you so adore with so much art—

TRISSOTIN

My mind speaks in those verses, not my heart.
I love those ladies in my poems merely,
While Henriette, alone, I love sincerely.

HENRIETTE

Please, Sir—

TRISSOTIN

If by so speaking I offend,
I fear that my offense will never end.
My ardor, which I've hidden hitherto,
Belongs for all eternity to you;

I'll love you till this beating heart has stopped;
And, though you scorn the tactics I adopt,
I can't refuse your mother's aid in gaining
The joy I'm so desirous of obtaining.
If the sweet prize I long for can be won,
And you be mine, I care not how it's done.

HENRIETTE

But don't you see that it's a risky course
To take possession of a heart by force;
That things, quite frankly, can go very ill
When a woman's made to wed against her will,
And that, in her resentment, she won't lack
For means to vex her spouse, and pay him back?

TRISSOTIN

I've no anxiety about such things.
The wise man takes whatever fortune brings.
Transcending vulgar weaknesses, his mind
Looks down unmoved on mishaps of the kind,
Nor does he feel the least distress of soul
Regarding matters not in his control.

HENRIETTE

You fascinate me, Sir; I'm much impressed.
I didn't know philosophy possessed
Such powers, and could teach men to endure
Such tricks of fate without discomfiture.
Your lofty patience ought, Sir, to be tested,
So that its greatness could be manifested;
It calls, Sir, for a wife who'd take delight
In making you display it, day and night;
But since I'm ill-equipped, by temperament,

To prove your virtue to its full extent,
I'll leave that joy to one more qualified,
And let some other woman be your bride.

TRISSOTIN

Well, we shall see. The notary for whom
Your mother sent is in the neighboring room.

SCENE TWO

_____

CHRYSALE, CLITANDRE,
MARTINE, HENRIETTE

CHRYSALE

Ah, Daughter, I'm pleased indeed to find you here.
Prepare to show obedience now, my dear,
By doing as your father bids you do.
I'm going to teach your mother a thing or two;
And, first of all, as you can see, I mean
To thwart her will and reinstate Martine.

HENRIETTE

I much admire the stands which you have taken.
Hold to them, Father; don't let yourself be shaken.
Be careful lest your kindly disposition
Induce you to abandon your position;
Cling to your resolutions, I entreat you,
And don't let Mother's stubbornness defeat you.

CHRYSALE

What! So you take me for a booby, eh?

HENRIETTE

Heavens, no!

CHRYSALE

Am I a milksop, would you say?

HENRIETTE

I'd not say that.

CHRYSALE

　　　　Do you think I lack the sense
To stand up firmly for my sentiments?

HENRIETTE

No, Father.

CHRYSALE

　　　　Have I too little brain and spirit
To run my own house? If so, let me hear it.

HENRIETTE

No, no.

CHRYSALE

　　　　Am I the sort, do you suppose,
Who'd let a woman lead him by the nose?

HENRIETTE

Of course not.

CHRYSALE

Well then, what were you implying?
Your doubts of me were scarcely gratifying.

HENRIETTE

I didn't mean to offend you, Heaven knows.

CHRYSALE

Under this roof, my girl, what I say goes.

HENRIETTE

True, Father.

CHRYSALE

No one but me has any right
To govern in this house.

HENRIETTE

Yes, Father; quite.

CHRYSALE

This is my family, and I'm sole head.

HENRIETTE

That's so.

CHRYSALE

I'll name the man my child shall wed.

HENRIETTE

Agreed!

CHRYSALE

By Heaven's laws, I rule your fate.

HENRIETTE

Who questions that?

CHRYSALE

And I'll soon demonstrate
That, in your marriage, your mother has no voice,
And that you must accept your father's choice.

HENRIETTE

Ah, Father, that's my dearest wish. I pray you,
Crown my desires by making me obey you.

CHRYSALE

If my contentious wife should dare to take—

CLITANDRE

She's coming, with the notary in her wake.

CHRYSALE

Stand by me, all of you.

MARTINE

Trust me, Sir. I'm here
To back you up, if need be. Never fear.

SCENE THREE

PHILAMINTE, BÉLISE, ARMANDE, TRISSOTIN,
THE NOTARY, CHRYSALE, CLITANDRE,
HENRIETTE, MARTINE

PHILAMINTE (*to the Notary*)

Can't you dispense with jargon, Sir, and write
Our contract in a style that's more polite?

THE NOTARY

Our style is excellent, Madam; I'd be absurd
Were I to modify a single word.

PHILAMINTE

Such barbarism, in the heart of France!
Can't you at least, for learning's sake, enhance
The document by putting the dowry down
In talent and drachma, rather than franc and crown?
And do use ides and calends for the date.

THE NOTARY

If I did, Madam, what you advocate,
I should invite professional ostracism.

PHILAMINTE

It's useless to contend with barbarism.
Come on, Sir; there's a writing table here.

[*Act Five · Scene Three*]

(*Noticing Martine*)
Ah! Impudent girl, how dare you reappear?
Why have you brought her back, Sir? Tell me why.

CHRYSALE

I'll tell you that at leisure, by and by.
First, there's another matter to decide.

THE NOTARY

Let us proceed with the contract. Where's the bride?

PHILAMINTE

I'm giving away my younger daughter.

THE NOTARY

I see.

CHRYSALE

Yes. Henriette's her name, Sir. This is she.

THE NOTARY

Good. And the bridegroom?

PHILAMINTE (*indicating Trissotin*)

This is the man I choose.

CHRYSALE (*indicating Clitandre*)

And I, for my part, have a bit of news:
This is the man she'll marry.

THE NOTARY

                         Two grooms? The law
Regards that as excessive.

PHILAMINTE

                  Don't hem and haw;
Just write down Trissotin, and your task is done.

CHRYSALE

Write down Clitandre; he's to be my son.

THE NOTARY

Kindly consult together, and agree
On a single person as the groom-to-be.

PHILAMINTE

No, no, Sir, do as I have indicated.

CHRYSALE

Come, come, put down the name that I have stated.

THE NOTARY

First tell me by whose orders I should abide.

PHILAMINTE (*to Chrysale*)

What's this, Sir? Shall my wishes be defied?

305

[*Act Five · Scene Three*]

CHRYSALE

I won't stand by and let this fellow take
My daughter's hand just for my money's sake.

PHILAMINTE

A lot your money matters to him! Indeed!
How dare you charge a learnèd man with greed?

CHRYSALE

Clitandre shall marry her, as I said before.

PHILAMINTE (*pointing to Trissotin*)

This is the man I've chosen. I'll hear no more.
The matter's settled, do you understand?

CHRYSALE

My! For a woman, you have a heavy hand.

MARTINE

It just ain't right for the wife to run the shop.
The man, I say, should always be on top.

CHRYSALE

Well said.

MARTINE

          Though I'm sacked ten times for saying so,
It's cocks, not hens, should be the ones to crow.

CHRYSALE

Correct.

MARTINE

When a man's wife wears the breeches, folks
Snicker about him, and make nasty jokes.

CHRYSALE

That's true.

MARTINE

If I had a husband, I wouldn't wish
For him to be all meek and womanish;
No, no, he'd be the captain of the ship,
And if I happened to give him any lip,
Or crossed him, he'd be right to slap my face
A time or two, to put me in my place.

CHRYSALE

Sound thinking.

MARTINE

The master's heart is rightly set
On finding a proper man for Henriette.

CHRYSALE

Yes.

MARTINE

Well then, here's Clitandre. Why deny
The girl a fine young chap like him? And why
Give her a learnèd fool who prates and drones?
She needs a husband, not some bag of bones
Who'll teach her Greek, and be her Latin tutor.
This Trissotin, I tell you, just don't suit her.

CHRYSALE

Right.

PHILAMINTE

We must let her chatter until she's through.

MARTINE

Talk, talk, is all these pedants know how to do.
If I ever took a husband, I've always said,
It wouldn't be no learnèd man I'd wed.
Wit's not the thing you need around the house,
And it's no joy to have a bookish spouse.
When I get married, you can bet your life
My man will study nothing but his wife;
He'll have no other book to read but me,
And won't—so please you, Ma'am—know A from B.

PHILAMINTE

Has your spokesman finished? And have I not politely
Listened to all her speeches?

CHRYSALE

The girl spoke rightly.

308

PHILAMINTE

Well then, to end all squabbling and delay,
Things now shall go exactly as I say.
(*Indicating Trissotin*)
Henriette shall wed this man at once, d'you hear?
Don't answer back; don't dare to interfere;
And if you've told Clitandre that he may wed
One of your daughters, give him Armande instead.

CHRYSALE

Well! . . . There's one way to settle this argument.
(*To Henriette and Clitandre*)
What do you think of that? Will you consent?

HENRIETTE

Oh, Father!

CLITANDRE

Oh, Sir!

BÉLISE

There's yet another bride
By whom he might be yet more satisfied;
But that can't be; the love we share is far
Higher and purer than the morning star;
Our bonds are solely of the intellect,
And all extended substance we reject.

SCENE FOUR

ARISTE, CHRYSALE, PHILAMINTE, BÉLISE,
HENRIETTE, ARMANDE, TRISSOTIN,
THE NOTARY, CLITANDRE, MARTINE

ARISTE

I hate to interrupt this happy affair
By bringing you the tidings which I bear.
You can't imagine what distress I feel
At the shocking news these letters will reveal.
                    (*To Philaminte*)
This one's from your attorney.
                    (*To Chrysale*)
                              And the other
Is yours; it's from Lyons.

CHRYSALE

                    What news, dear Brother,
Could be so pressing, and distress you so?

ARISTE

There is your letter; read it, and you'll know.

PHILAMINTE (*reading*)

"Madam, I have asked your brother to convey to you this
message, advising you of something which I dared not come

and tell you in person. Owing to your great neglect of your affairs, the magistrate's clerk did not notify me of the preliminary hearing, and you have irrevocably lost your lawsuit, which you should in fact have won."

CHRYSALE (*to Philaminte*)

You've lost your case!

PHILAMINTE

My! Don't be shaken so!
I'm not disheartened by this trivial blow.
Do teach your heart to take a nobler stance
And brave, like me, the buffetings of chance.

"This negligence of yours has cost you forty thousand crowns, for it is that amount, together with the legal expenses, which the court has condemned you to pay."

Condemned! What shocking language! That's a word
Reserved for criminals.

ARISTE

True; your lawyer erred,
And you're entirely right to be offended.
He should say that the court has *recommended*
That you comply with its decree, and pay
Forty thousand and costs without delay.

PHILAMINTE

What's in this other letter?

CHRYSALE (*reading*)

"Sir, my friendship with your brother leads me to take an interest in all that concerns you. I know that you have

put your money in the hands of Argante and Damon, and
I regret to inform you that they have both, on the same day,
gone into bankruptcy."

Lost! All my money! Every penny of it!

PHILAMINTE

What a shameful outburst, Sir. Come, rise above it!
The wise man doesn't mourn the loss of pelf;
His wealth lies not in things, but in himself.
Let's finish this affair, with no more fuss:
(*Pointing to Trissotin*)
His fortune will suffice for all of us.

TRISSOTIN

No, Madam, urge my cause no further. I see
That everyone's against this match and me,
And where I am not wanted, I shan't intrude.

PHILAMINTE

Well! That's a sudden change of attitude.
It follows close on our misfortunes, Sir.

TRISSOTIN

Weary of opposition, I prefer
To bow out gracefully, and to decline
A heart which will not freely yield to mine.

PHILAMINTE

I see now what you are, Sir. I perceive
What, till this moment, I would not believe.

TRISSOTIN

See what you like; I do not care one whit
What you perceive, or what you think of it.
I've too much self-respect to tolerate
The rude rebuffs I've suffered here of late:
Men of my worth should not be treated so:
Thus slighted, I shall make my bow, and go.
                    (*He leaves.*)

PHILAMINTE

What a low-natured, mercenary beast!
He isn't philosophic in the least!

CLITANDRE

Madam, I'm no philosopher; but still
I beg to share your fortunes, good or ill,
And dare to offer, together with my hand,
The little wealth I happen to command.

PHILAMINTE

This generous gesture, Sir, I much admire,
And you deserve to have your heart's desire.
I grant your suit, Sir. Henriette and you—

HENRIETTE

No, Mother, I've changed my mind. Forgive me, do,
If once more I oppose your plans for me.

CLITANDRE

What! Will you cheat me of felicity,
Now that the rest have yielded, one and all?

HENRIETTE

I know, Clitandre, that your wealth is small.
I wished to marry you so long as I
Might realize my sweetest hopes thereby,
And at the same time mend your circumstances.
But after this great blow to our finances,
I love you far too deeply to impose
On you the burden of our present woes.

CLITANDRE

I welcome any fate which you will share,
And any fate, without you, I couldn't bear.

HENRIETTE

So speaks the reckless heart of love; but let's
Be prudent, Sir, and thus avoid regrets.
Nothing so strains the bond of man and wife
As lacking the necessities of life,
And in the end, such dull and mean vexations
Can lead to quarrels and recriminations.

ARISTE (*to Henriette*)

Is there any reason, save the one you've cited,
Why you and Clitandre shouldn't be united?

HENRIETTE

But for that cause, I never would say no;
I must refuse because I love him so.

ARISTE

Then let the bells ring out for him and you.
The bad news which I brought was all untrue.

314

'Twas but a stratagem which I devised
In hopes to see your wishes realized
And undeceive my sister, showing her
The baseness of her pet philosopher.

CHRYSALE

Now, Heaven be praised for that!

PHILAMINTE

                I'm overjoyed
To think how that false wretch will be annoyed,
And how the rich festivities of this
Glad marriage will torment his avarice.

CHRYSALE (*to Clitandre*)

Well, Son, our firmness has achieved success.

ARMANDE (*to Philaminte*)
Shall you sacrifice me to their happiness?

PHILAMINTE

Daughter, your sacrifice will not be hard.
Philosophy will help you to regard
Their wedded joys with equanimity.

BÉLISE

Let him be careful lest his love for me
Drive him, in desperation, to consent
To a rash marriage of which he will repent.

[*Act Five · Scene Four*]

CHRYSALE (*to the Notary*)

Come, come, Sir, it is time your task was through;
Draw up the contract just as I told you to.

New and Collected Poems
The Poems of Richard Wilbur

TRANSLATIONS.

Molière's *Amphitryon*
Molière's *The Misanthrope* and *Tartuffe*
Molière's *The School for Husbands* and *Sganarelle*
Molière's *The School for Wives* and *The Learned Ladies*
Molière's *Tartuffe*
Racine's *Andromache*
Racine's *Phaedra*